Indo-Asiatische Zeitschrift

Mitteilungen der Gesellschaft für indo-asiatische Kunst

26 · 2022

Inhalt / Contents

Vorwort / Foreword 2

A Different Approach and a New Home for the Museum für Asiatische Kunst
Raffael Dedo Gadebusch 4

With Drumbeats to the Buddhahood: Drummers in the Barrel Vault Paintings of the Buddhist Cave Temples of Ancient Kucha
Ji Ho Yi 13

Die Konservierung und Restaurierung von Wandmalereien aus der Studiensammlung des Museums für Asiatische Kunst, Berlin
Marie Fortmann, Angela Mitschke, Joana Schaer 23

„Für die Seele meines Vaters ...Kara Totok" – Die Darstellung eines hohen, uigurischen Würdenträgers auf einer Tempelfahne aus Kocho
Thomas Arens 30

A 'Pensive Bodhisatva' from Takht-i-Bahi, Formerly in the Museum für Völkerkunde, Berlin: Object History and Art Historical Study
Corinna Wessels-Mevissen 36

An Enigmatic Performer in Ajanta
Mercedes Tortorici 52

The Great Blue – Tiles from Punjab on Display in the Museum für Asiatische Kunst at the Humboldt Forum, Berlin.
Dorina Michaelis 59

Die Umāmaheśvara-Stele von Chatrarhi: Das 3D-Modell als Studienobjekt
Gerald Kozicz 69

Religious Transfer from India to the Mekong Delta – Three Different Cases Documented by Images
Adalbert J. Gail 77

Ein neuer Player in Dahlem – Der Forschungscampus der SPK
Alexis von Poser & Patricia Rahemipour 84

Jahresrückblick 2022
Dörte Eriskat & Uta Schröder 86

Autoren / Contributors 2022 89

Mitglieder der Gesellschaft für indo-asiatische Kunst 2022 91

Impressum / Imprint 96

Vorwort / Foreword

Liebe Freunde, liebe Förderer unseres Museums,

wenn Sie dieses Heft in Händen halten, wird unser Museum im Humboldt Forum endlich vollständig geöffnet sein. Mehr Ausstellungsfläche, mehr Objekte, mehr Kontext und noch mehr moderne und zeitgenössische Kunst – über das neue, innovative Konzept unseres Hauses am prominenten Standort in der Mitte Berlins informiert der Beitrag von Raffael Dedo Gadebusch.

Alexis von Poser und Patricia Rahemipour zeigen ferner auf, was für den „alten" Standort in Dahlem geplant ist. Auch hier wird es spannende Entwicklungen geben.

Das Thema Wandmalerei bildet einen Schwerpunkt dieser Ausgabe. Dabei berichtet Ji Ho Yi über Ihre Arbeit zu Wandmalereien in Kucha und Mercedes Tortorici interpretiert eine Malerei in Ajanta. Der Artikel von Marie Fortmann, Angela Mitschke und Joana Schaer widmet sich der Konservierung und Restaurierung von Wandmalereien in unserem Museum. Dieses Thema gibt gleichsam einen Ausblick darauf, was Sie im vollständig eröffneten Museum für Asiatische Kunst erwartet. Die restauratorische Arbeit an den Objekten der Sammlung wird in dem Artikel von Thomas Arens, Restaurator der umfangreichen und bedeutenden Textilsammlungen des Museums, an einem Fallbeispiel anschaulich gemacht.

Weitere Artikel widmen sich dem Kulturtransfer im weitesten Sinne, wobei einmal mehr die außerordentliche Spannweite der für unsere Gesellschaft relevanten Themen deutlich wird:

Corinna Wessels-Mevissen geht von einem „nachdenklichen Bodhisatva" aus und verweist auf kunsthistorische Verbindungen bis zum Mittelmeerraum, während Adalbert Gail solche bei hinduistischen Darstellungen von Indien bis zum Mekong-Delta aufzeigt. Dorina Michaelis widmet sich dem islamischen Einfluss auf die

Dear friends of Indo-Asian art, dear patrons,

When you hold this issue in your hands, our museum will have finally be opened. More exhibition space, more art objects, more context and even more modern and contemporary art – the article by Raffael Dedo Gadebusch informs you about the new, innovative concept of our house at the prominent location in the centre of Berlin.

Alexis von Poser and Patricia Rahemipour further show what is planned at the "old" location in Dahlem. Here, too, there will be exciting developments.

The theme of mural paintings is a focus of this issue. Ji Ho Yi reports on her work on murals in Kucha and Mercedes Tortorici interprets a painting in Ajanta. The article by Marie Fortmann, Angela Mitschke and Joana Schaer is dedicated to the conservation and restoration of mural paintings in our museum. This also gives a preview, of what will await you in the fully opened Museum of Asian Art. The article by Thomas Arens, a conservator of the museum's extensive and important textile collections, uses a case study to illustrate the restoration work on objects in the collection.

Other articles are devoted to cultural transfer in the broadest sense, once again highlighting the extraordinary range of issues relevant to our society:

Corinna Wessels-Mevissen discusses a "pensive Bodhisatva" and points to art historical connections as far as to the Mediterranean, while Adalbert Gail shows such connections in Hindu representations from India to the Mekong Delta. Dorina Michaelis focuses on the Islamic influence on the art of the Indian subcontinent and introduces us to the tradition of blue and white glazed tiles in the Punjab.

Finally, the contribution by Gerald Kozicz uses a stele from Himachal Pradesh to show the possibilities offered by digitalization of works of art.

Kunst des indischen Subkontinents und führt uns ein in die Tradition blau-weiß glasierter Fliesen im Punjab.

Schließlich zeigt der Beitrag von Gerald Kozicz anhand einer Stele aus Himachal Pradesh, welche Möglichkeiten die digitale Erfassung von Kunstwerken bietet.

Auch die Gesellschaft für indo-asiatische Kunst setzt auf Digitalisierung und digitale Kommunikation, ohne jedoch ihre anlogen Stärken aufzugeben. Bitte nutzen Sie auch unsere Homepage giak.org, auf der wir ein Diskussionsforum für Mitglieder eingerichtet haben.

Prof. Dr. Felix Gross, Vorsitzender der Gesellschaft für indo-asiatische Kunst und *Raffael Dedo Gadebusch*, Leiter des Museums für Asiatische Kunst

The Society for Indo-Asian Art also relies on digitalization and digital communication, but without giving up its analogous strengths. Please also use our homepage giak.org, where we have set up a new discussion forum for members.

Prof. Dr. Felix Gross, Chairman of the Society for Indo-Asian Art and *Raffael Dedo Gadebusch*, Head of the Asian Art Museum Berlin

A Different Approach and a New Home for the Museum für Asiatische Kunst

Raffael Dedo Gadebusch

In 2002 the German parliament made the decision to "rebuild" the Berlin Palace of the house of Hohenzollern, the royal dynasty that ruled Germany until the end of world war I, reconstructing its Baroque façades on three sides of the building and within the eastern courtyard (**Fig. 1**). Discussions about the resurrection of this palace were highly controversial, being related to the problematic history of imperial Germany around the year 1900. The Stiftung Preußischer Kulturbesitz (SPK), in charge of the Prussian cultural assets held and shown today in museums, archives and libraries across Berlin, was smart to propose an exclusively cultural use for the disputed building. The idea of making its world-famous collections from Asia, Africa, Oceania, and the Americas – at that time still housed in the Museum für Asiatische Kunst (Asian Art Museum) and the Ethnologisches Museum (Ethnological Museum) in the elegant suburban district of Dahlem – the core of a newly established institution seemed a smart move to silence the many critical voices regarding the idea of a replica of an Imperial palace. A centre for arts, culture and learning with a clear focus beyond the Old World represented on the Museum Island, was the declared goal. The institution is named after the famous scholars and brothers Wilhelm (1767–1835) and Alexander (1769–1859) von Humboldt. During the years since the initial planning, the concept for the Humboldt Forum was modified a few times. Institutions like the Berlin Public Library, which was supposed to become a key player to attract primarily Berliners, found another location, and the Stadtmuseum (Museum of the City of Berlin) together with Kulturprojekte Berlin moved in. Another protagonist is the Humboldt University with its "Humboldt Lab", showing the relevance of scholarship and curatorial work for topical issues and current global debates. Eventually the different institutions coexist rather than form a unity with a common approach. The Stiftung Humboldt Forum is the entity that owns and operates the building and is the coordinator of the interests of all the players within. It also maintains a permanent exhibition of the history of the site.

Fig. 1 View of the Berlin Palace, towards the east and north façade © Stiftung Humboldt Forum im Berliner Schloss / Photo: Alexander Schippel

The third floor of the Humboldt Forum is entirely dedicated to the arts and cultures of Asia. The Museum für Asiatische Kunst occupies the third floor's west wing, which includes the impressive octagonal hall underneath the palace cupola, and a small part of the east wing. The west wing opened its doors in autumn 2021. For additional exhibition space, the architect Franco Stella added two huge cubic buildings to the west wing, set within the western courtyard, but directly attached to the historic ground plan, which provide more exhibition space for permanent displays. The galleries of the Museum für Asiatische Kunst occupy two big halls, which are part of those additions. In fact, the museum's new exhibition space designed by the renowned architecture firm Ralph Appelbaum Associates is much larger than its old premises in Dahlem. Another advantage to the new location is the arrangement of all the galleries on a single floor, which not only makes a visit much easier but also interconnects the galleries of the former Museum für Ostasiatische Kunst (Museum of East Asian Art) and the Museum für Indische Kunst (Museum of Indian Art), which were merged in 2006 into the Museum für Asiatische Kunst.

The arts especially from South Asia and from Southeast Asia received additional exhibition space. The Southeast Asian galleries, which opened in September 2022 are located in the east wing of the building, near the permanent exhibition spaces of the Ethnologisches Museum with its collections from the same region. Manuscripts, stone sculptures, bronzes and architectural ornaments from Thailand, Myanmar, Cambodia (**Fig. 2**) and the Indonesian archipelago reflect the many centuries lasting impact of Indian culture and religion in those regions. The artworks on display are contextualized not only through wall texts, images and illustrations as well as interactive media applications but also through a huge wooden model of the Angkor Wat as well as the famous Berlin replicas of the reliefs from the same temple based on moulds from the 19th century.

In the South Asian art galleries, far more objects are on display than ever before, especially in the field of early Buddhist art from the Gandharan region (**Fig. 3**). The museum holdings in this area are particularly rich, regarding quantity as well as quality. Group presentations of Buddha images in stone and in stucco are a new approach compared to the more minimalist presentation in the past. Of special importance is the huge collection of stucco objects from Gandhara, which offer an idea of the many stylistic varieties within the early mass production of Buddhist cult images.

Fig. 2 Eight-headed dancing Hevajra, Cambodia, 12th–13th century CE, bronze. Museum für Asiatische Kunst, Acc. No. II 1138 © Staatliche Museen zu Berlin, Museum für Asiatische Kunst / Jürgen Liepe

Bountiful installations can also be found in other galleries. The most impressive example is the new presentation of the Central Asian collection in two large galleries, under the dome and located in the cubic building, respectively. The many art works from the northern Silk Road, first of all the splendid and well preserved early (mainly) Buddhist wall paintings and clay sculptures – once housed in the storerooms of the Dahlem site and therefore accessible only to specialists – are now on view permanently, which means that a notable part of the museum is now a study collection open to everybody (**Fig. 4**). This new concept, hardly seen elsewhere in Europe, represents a big step towards becoming a more transparent institution. Visitors will encounter other rich presentations or publicly accessible study collections in the gal-

Fig. 3 Buddha (Pakistan, 2nd–3rd century) in the gallery Buddhist Art in South Asia. Stupas, Buddhas, Bodhisattvas *© Staatliche Museen zu Berlin / Stiftung Humboldt Forum im Berliner Schloss / Photo: Alexander Schippel*

leries of courtly Indian art and in the Chinese and Korean art galleries. Transparency is an important part of the museum's philosophy, and it becomes apparent not least through gallery texts that make provenance an important subject of discussion. All object labels mention at least the most recent owner of the work on display. This paradigm shift reflects the current debates on the provenance of items in public institutions. The history of ownership, always a topic for art historians, has become increasingly related to considerations on power relationships between people. Since a significant number of artworks had been acquired during the period of colonial rule (this applies, above all, to objects from South and Southeast Asia), the Museum für Asiatische Kunst promotes an open debate regarding misdemeanours in the time of colonialism in connection with its acquisitions. Therefore, new results of provenance research will be presented continuously in the galleries.

There are more aspects that make the Museum für Asiatische Kunst a museum of today. Once primarily an institution for connoisseurs, where artworks were arranged by material and genre or shown chronologically, based on a classical art-historical approach, the new museum presents its collections to visitors mainly through strong narrative frameworks. This makes the objects on view far more accessible to a broader audience. That the Museum für Asiatische Kunst moved from the outskirts to the very centre of Berlin also helps in this effort. More than ever before, the artworks on display are explained through the contexts in which they were produced and used. Buddhist and Jain sculptures or Hindu and Vedic cult images from South Asia can be enjoyed for their outstanding craftsmanship, their elegant form, their particular iconography, but they can only be understood more fully when their meaning and function in ritual is explained, with an introduction to culture, religion, and philosophy of the region. This applies particularly to the complex iconographies of Hindu images (**Fig. 5**). In the South and Southeast Asian galleries special attention is paid therefore to educational approaches. The amount of information in the wall texts and object labels is far more comprehensive than in previous presentations. Film clips explain the complex iconographies of religious artworks, and visitors can broaden their knowledge through interactive media stations, which can also be found throughout the museum. Eventually a Family Trail with specially designed furniture invites families to linger in the galleries.

Collecting and showing modern and contemporary art has been part of the concept of the Museum für Asiatische Kunst since its inception, and, in the Humboldt Forum, contemporary artworks are also part of the new design. The large-scale video-and-sound installation "Gardens in the Sky" by the New York based artist Alexander Gorlizki and the composer Richard Coldman creates a dialogue with the works on display in the gallery dedicated to the arts of courtly India; traditional Indian-miniature painters were involved in the creation of the images used in the video projection. In the gallery of arts from Japan Jun Ura and Ura Architects and Engineers, together with the tea master Sōkyū Nara and the artists Syouitsu (Shōitsu) Nishimura III, Takuo Nakamura, and Naoki Sakai, all from Kanazawa, created a contemporary version of a traditional Japanese tea house, which is the centrepiece of the section on the practice of the "way of tea" (**Fig. 6**).

Fig. 4 Exhibition view of the domed room in the gallery Turfan Collection Central Asia © *Staatliche Museen zu Berlin / Stiftung Humboldt Forum im Berliner Schloss / Photo: Alexander Schippel*

Fig. 5 View into the gallery Hindu Art in South Asia © *Staatliche Museen zu Berlin / Stiftung Humboldt Forum im Berliner Schloss / Photo: Alexander Schippel*

Fig. 6 The tea house developed by URA Architects from Kanazawa (Japan) in close coordination with the Chado Urasenke Teeweg Association in Berlin in the gallery Art in Japan (area: Tea as Art) © *Staatliche Museen zu Berlin / Stiftung Humboldt Forum im Berliner Schloss / Photo: Alexander Schippel*

Certainly, the most stunning contemporary intervention in the Museum is the creation of the Chinese architect Wang Shu, winner of the prestigious Pritzker Architecture Prize in 2012. Wang designed the gallery of Chinese court art and was involved in the selection of the objects for this gallery (**Fig. 7**). The cooperation with an important representative of contemporary Chinese art and architecture on this particular gallery is pioneering and even groundbreaking, as the gallery presents the complex and fruitful but also problematic encounters of Europe and China during the rule of the Qing dynasty (1644–1911).

Contemporary interventions in the South Asian galleries of Buddhist, Jain, and Hindu art have yet to materialize, but an important criterion for future acquisitions will be the ability of modern or contemporary works of art to enter into dialogue with the objects on display or to refer to the narratives of the exhibitions. Alexander Gorlizki's video installation perfectly fulfils this criterion as it was realized over a period of three years in close cooperation with the curator of the gallery. The textile onto which the moving images are projected suggests a canopy, like those used on courtly garden terraces often seen in Mughal-style paintings; museum visitors will encounter such paintings in the gallery. Also the partly abstract, partly figurative imagery projected on the lower part of the baldachin structure refers to specific objects and the narrative of the exhibition: the Indo-Persian garden as a leitmotif of Indian court life during Mughal rule (**Fig. 8**).

Fig. 7 View into the gallery of Chinese Court Art *designed by Chinese architect Wang Shu © Staatliche Museen zu Berlin / Stiftung Humboldt Forum im Berliner Schloss / Photo: Alexander Schippel*

Fig. 8 View into the gallery Courtly India *with the video installation by Alexander Gorlizki © Staatliche Museen zu Berlin / Stiftung Humboldt Forum im Berliner Schloss / Photo: Alexander Schippel*

Fig. 9 View into the gallery Turfan Collection Central Asia © *Staatliche Museen zu Berlin / Stiftung Humboldt Forum im Berliner Schloss / Photo: Alexander Schippel*

Geometric clarity and symmetry play a key role in Islamic architecture and art. This aesthetic shift in Indian art is reflected in the exhibition design, contrasting with the gallery of Hindu art nearby. The positioning of the gallery of courtly India within the museum's floor plan reflects also the chronology of Indian art, to a certain extent, as it follows the gallery of Hindu art in the southwest corner of the west wing, which the visitor enters after being in the huge gallery of Buddhist and Jain art that begins the museum's tour of South Asia.

In the impressive gallery underneath the dome of the palace, the installation of objects from the Central Asian collection connects South to East Asia, as ideas and religions and their artistic expressions travelled along those ancient trade routes, called Silk Roads. In the gallery, an abstract landscape evokes the caves in the steep cliffs in Kizil, where many of the museum's famous wall paintings were discovered, and functions as a shell for a partly reconstructed Buddhist cave (**Fig. 9**). Images from the Buddhist caves in Kizil as well as images that refer to the movements on the Silk Roads are projected onto the ceiling of the room.

A common thread connecting South and East Asia is Buddhism. The neighbouring gallery therefore addresses the subject of pilgrimage, showing masterpieces of sacred art from India, Central Asia, China, and Japan, whereas Tantric Buddhist art from the Himalayan region, the roof of the world, is on display on an elevated gallery in the cubic hall where the bigger part of the Central Asian collection is on view. Important Tangkas from Tibet and Nepal, ritual bronzes as well as rare wooden sculptures from Nepal are among the highlights of the Himalayan collection (**Fig. 10**).

Fig. 10 Cintāmani Lokeśvara, Nepal, 15th–16th century, wood with traces of paint. Museum für Asiatische Kunst, Acc. No. I 10070 © Staatliche Museen zu Berlin, Museum für Asiatische Kunst / Jürgen Liepe

Continuing the tour towards the north, coming from the hall underneath the dome of the palace, visitors enter the gallery of the arts of Japan. Its rather intimate spaces are dedicated to museum benefactors Klaus F. and Yoshie Naumann (**Fig. 11**). Emphasizing the enormous diversity of creative expressions in Japan, the presentation adopts a thematic approach and focuses on issues such as: the function of framing devices like display alcoves (tokonoma); the interplay of writing, painting, and performing arts; the function of formats such as screens in the creation of spaces. Regular rotations of the works on display will add other thematic layers.

The following so-called Transregional Thematic Exhibition Gallery is a new innovative feature in the museum. It connects Japan with Korea and China. Functioning as an interface between all three cultures, it provides the possibility of cross-cultural exhibitions that concern the arts of entire East Asia.

Contemporary art is the focus of the Korean Gallery in the Humboldt Forum. Since the Korean collection is quite limited in terms of quantity, the curatorial decision was to show almost all light-insensitive artworks, mostly ceramics and bronzes, in a clustered presentation or study collection, which is in line with the overall concept of the transparent museum. What is unusual is the decision to also including the historical practice of packaging by showing the wood storage boxes specially made for the fragile ceramics, which helps the visitor to consider aspects of collecting and storing.

The last two galleries of the round tour are dedicated to the arts of China. (Visitors could also begin their itinerary from here and move towards South Asia.)

The collection of Chinese art, including ancient bronzes, ceramics, lacquerware and furniture, unlike in Dahlem where the collection was displayed according to classification and mostly also chronologically, is now dis-

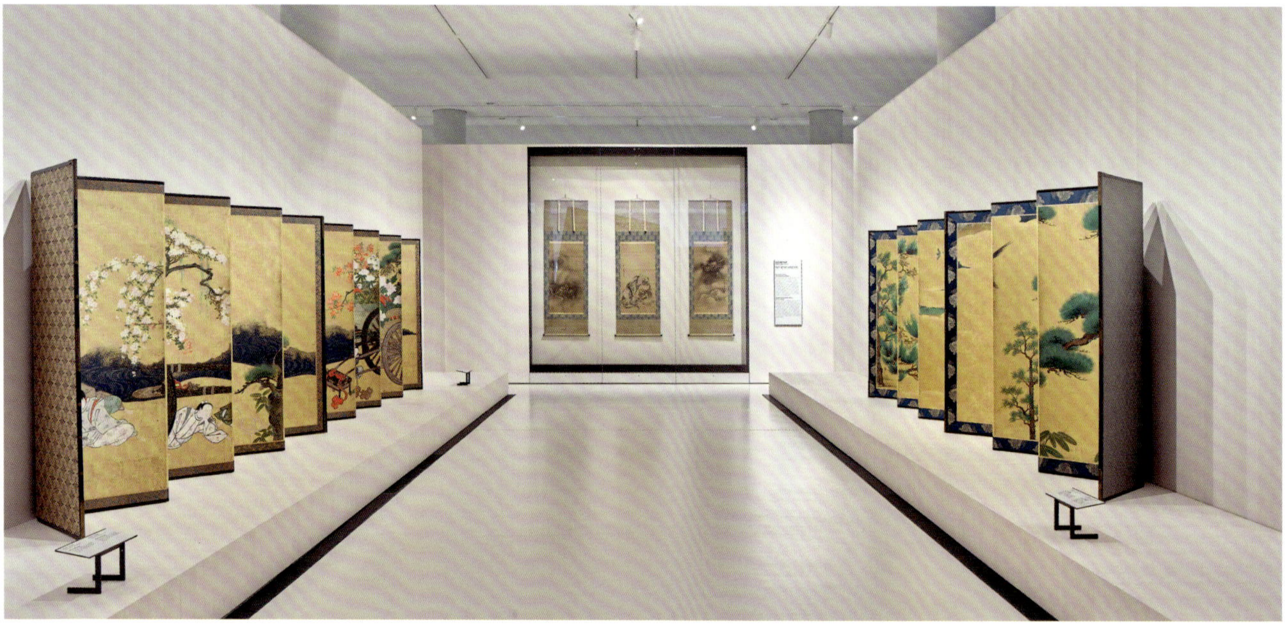

Fig. 11 View into the gallery Art in Japan (area: Painting and Space) © *Staatliche Museen zu Berlin / Stiftung Humboldt Forum im Berliner Schloss / Photo: Alexander Schippel*

played in one space to provide a better understanding of the environment of Chinese scholars and their collecting, study and artistic practices. While the study collection of ceramics provides an overview of local production and international trade, the rotation of light-sensitive objects such as paintings and calligraphies offer regularly new small thematic exhibitions on relevant themes in the visual arts of China (**Fig. 12**).

Fig. 12 View into the gallery Chinese Art in Context: Artists and Connoisseurs *with the* East Asia Study Collection © *Staatliche Museen zu Berlin / Stiftung Humboldt Forum im Berliner Schloss / Foto: Alexander Schippel*

The other gallery dedicated to Chinese art is the hall conceived by Wang Shu, mentioned above. Considering its sophisticated and unusual design, it can be considered one of the highlights not only of the Museum für Asiatische Kunst but also of the entire Humboldt Forum.

This article is based on a contribution in *Orientations* Vol. 53 No.2 (March/April 2022) by the same author on occasion of the opening of the first part of the Museum für Asiatische Kunst in the Humboldt Forum.

With Drumbeats to the Buddhahood: Drummers in the Barrel Vault Paintings of the Buddhist Cave Temples of Ancient Kucha

Ji Ho Yi

One of the conspicuous features in the paintings that decorate the Buddhist monastic grottoes of Kucha is the image of musicians on the walls' upper register. The various images of heavenly musicians holding musical instruments in Kizil Cave 38 are vital works, with the allusion to music as their crucial element. This inclusion of musicians is not surprising when we consider that Kucha is known to have been famous for its musical performances with string and pipe, as recorded at the time of the monk pilgrim Xuanzang (602–664 CE).[1] Yet, beyond this connection to documented musical performances, a closer look at the paintings reveals that music is not only represented through the image of musicians that makes viewers imagine the melodies played inside the cave. Among the 2nd Indo-Iranian Style narrative paintings in the barrel vaults, there are a few instances where a drummer is shown face to face with a seated Buddha. These comprise two types: In one, the drummer is a child, recognisable by his nakedness, who beats a barrel drum with a stick in one of his hands; in the other type, an adult drummer beats an hourglass drum with his hands. The illustration of these stories in the barrel vaults of the Kucha caves implies that the music offering was regarded as appropriate to venerate the Buddha. While these images provide clues about the Kucha people's interest in musical performance, they also tell us something about their religious background, as these image types are based on two different stories preserved in Chinese translations of the *Mūlasarvāstivāda-vinaya*.

Beginning with the source for the first type of image, the story of the child drummer survived in two texts related to the Mūlasarvāstivāda school. The first is the *Mūlasarvāstivāda-vinaya* (*T* 1442: 835a13–c9); the English translation of the relevant passage by the present author is appended to this article. The other text is the *Mūlasarvāstivādin Precepts for Nuns* (*T* 1443: 984b1–985a6). In the early 8th century, the monk Yijing (635–713 CE) translated these two texts into Chinese. The existence of the Sanskrit, Pali, Tocharian, or Tibetan version of this story is yet to be proven.[2] According to the story, the Buddha and the monks meet two children at the entrance of a village. In *T* 1442, the children offer to guide the group, with one boy leading the group and beating a drum and the other protecting the group from behind with a bow and arrow. In *T* 1443, the children do not offer a guide but honour the Buddha with music: One boy beats the drum, and the other plucks the bow as if playing a stringed instrument. After the Buddha dismisses them, he smiles and radiates light. The Buddha tells Ānanda that, after being reborn as humans and gods (*deva*) in thirteen *kalpa*s, the boys will attain the peerless, correct, perfect enlightenment in their final life. The boy with the drum will become Dharma-drum-sound-Tathāgata, and the one with the bow will be-

1 *T* 2087, ed. vol. 51: 870a17–21. The English translation in Beal 1884: I, 19 wrote "They excel other countries in their skill in playing on the lute and pipe".

2 While further research is needed, these stories were not included in the *Bhikṣuprātimokṣa* of the Sarvāstivāda school translated by Rosen in 1959, nor in the translation of the narratives from Tibetan *Mūlasarvāstivāda-vinaya* by Panglung in 1981. There are also the fragments of Tocharian B texts of *vinaya* and *avadāna* stories continually being translated, but there were yet no matching story with the child and adult drummers in those works. See CEToM webpage at https://www.univie.ac.at/tocharian/?search (accessed May 2022) and the works of Hirotoshi Ogihara for *vinaya* and *avadāna* stories in Tocharian B including those in the bibliography of this article. An overview of the surviving canonical literature and the related researches concerning Sarvāstivāda and Mūlasarvāstivāda schools are well summarised in Oberlies 2003: 45–71. It is possible that there is a matching piece in Sanskrit and other languages among the surviving literature.

come Bestowing-fearlessness-Tathāgata. Illustrations of this story have been found in five caves in the territory of ancient Kucha: Kizil Cave 8 (**Fig. 1**),[3] Kizil Cave 184,[4] Kizil Cave 186 (**Fig. 2**),[5] Kizilgaha Cave 23,[6] and Simsim Cave 30.[7] In the case of Kizil Cave 8, MA identified this image as the illustration of the story described in *T* 152 of a boy playing with the rattle drum made of the skin of a bull, which he himself was in his former life.[8] In the story, the Buddha was Indra, who transformed himself into a merchant to meet his old friend, the lady shopkeeper, at the market. This identification was reconfirmed by MA and FAN in 2007.[9] The rattle drum has a handle and two tiny knobs fastened with strings that both hit the sides of the drum when the drummer revolves the handle, whereas the drum in the picture is a barrel drum with an independent stick. Moreover, the Buddha does not appear in the story because he was in the guise of a merchant. For these reasons, it seems more likely that the story of the child drummer guiding the Buddha from *T* 1442 was illustrated in Kizil Cave 8, rather than the other story from *T* 152.

Examples from Kizil Cave 8 (**Fig. 1**) and Kizilgaha Cave 23 depict the boy on the left side of the picture kneeling on one leg and beating a barrel drum with a raised drumstick in one hand. The examples from Kizil Cave 186 (**Fig. 2**) and Simsim Cave 30 show a boy standing on the right side of the picture, with his body forming a soft S-curve. The boy in the painting from Kizil Cave 184 seems to be standing in a similar pose to those from

Fig. 1 Child drummer and Buddha. Kizil Cave 8 (Sechzehnschwertträgerhöhle), main chamber, barrel vault, left haunch, 3rd register, no. 7, in situ. After Kizil Grottoes 1983–1985/1989–1997: I, pl. 35

Kizil Cave 186 and Simsim Cave 30, but as his lower body is damaged it is impossible to figure out the exact posture. The barrel drum held by the boy seems adequate to warn the possible spectators and clear the way while leading the group.

Although the child bowman mentioned in the texts is absent in all illustrations of the child drummer, there are independent depictions of archers found in Kucha. In Kizil Cave 186, the painting on the right side of the rear lunette depicts a Buddha with a bowman. It is on the same lunette where the Buddha and a child drummer are painted on the left side, although the two scenes are not arranged to be exactly opposite each other.[10] However, as

3 Kizil Cave 8 (Sechzehnschwertträgerhöhle), main chamber, barrel vault, left haunch, 3rd register, no. 7, *in situ*. Illustrated on a historical photograph taken on the third German expedition in 1906, kept in the Museum für Asiatische Kunst, Berlin, no. B 621; on a historical photograph taken on the French expedition in 1907, kept in the Musée Guimet, Paris, no. AP7464; in *Kizil Grottoes* 1983–1985/1989–1997: I, pls. 27, 35; MA/FAN 2007: 176–177; *ZXBQ* 2008: 138–139, pl. 122; *ZXBY* 2009: II, 288–289, pl. 257.

4 Kizil Cave 184 (Drittletzte Höhle, 2. Schlucht), main chamber, rear lunette, left side, *in situ*. Illustrated in *ZXBY* 2009: III, 123, 125–126, pls. 107, 109–110.

5 Kizil Cave 186 (Mittlere Höhle, 2. Schlucht), main chamber, rear lunette, left side, *in situ*. Illustrated in TAN/AN 1981: II, pl. 116; *ZXBY* 2009: III, 145, 148, pls. 126, 129.

6 Kizilgaha Cave 23, main chamber, barrel vault, right haunch, 3rd register, no. 1, *in situ*.

7 Simsim Cave 30, main chamber, barrel vault, left haunch, register and number unclear, *in situ*. Here the boy's left hand seems to hold the stick, although it is faded.

8 MA 1984: 215; MA 1996: 210; *T* 152: 37b23–38a9.

9 MA/FAN 2007: 176–177. However, *T* 152 has been misinterpreted here by taking the boy with the rattle drum as identical to the other boy in the story, who was the father of the lady shopkeeper in his former life.

10 Kizil Cave 186 (Mittlere Höhle, 2. Schlucht), main chamber, rear lunette, right side, *in situ*. Illustrated in *ZXBY* 2009: III, 145, 149, pls. 126, 130.

Fig. 2 Child drummer and Buddha. Kizil Cave 186 (Mittlere Höhle, 2. Schlucht), main chamber, rear lunette, left side, in situ. After Tan/An *1981: II, pl. 116*

the archer wears short pants, he seems to be an adult, because children are usually depicted naked, although they are often wearing ornaments, in Kucha wall paintings. On the left haunch of the barrel vault of the Simsim Cave 30, there is an example of a narrative painting with a child bowman, but the animal on the other side of the Buddha may indicate that an entirely different story is represented here.[11] The narrative scene with the child drummer was also on the left haunch of the barrel vault in the same cave, but the exact locations of the two depictions of the child archer and child drummer are unknown, therefore it is impossible to figure out whether they were located next to each other. Given that these rare representations of archers, especially child archers, are located in the same caves as the drummer illustrations, it is possible that these archers also allude to the same narrative, or the two different stories featuring children who later became a Buddha could have circulated in Kucha at the same time and later merged into one story as the version surviving in Yijing's translations from 8th century CE.

Turning to the source for the second type of image, the story of the adult drummer appears in the *Saṅghabhedavastu* of the Chinese *Mūlasarvāstivāda-vinaya* (*T* 1450: 190c13–191b26), again connected with the Mūlasarvāstivāda school as the story of child drummer. The story itself is introduced with a background account explaining that King Bimbisāra had to meet a tragic death due to his terrible deed in a former life. Following this, the story continues that King Ajātaśatru, the son of Bimbisāra, was devastated to hear of his father's death. As King Ajātaśatru was inconsolable, his attendants invited a musician from Southern India who came to Magadha to the royal palace. Still, the king was unhappy and ignored the musician, who left the palace and went to the Buddha's place. The musician greeted him and was delighted. He played the drum and made music, at which point the Buddha smiled and shined the light. The Buddha told Ānanda that the musician would become a *pratyekabuddha* in the future, known as the Gracious-harmonious-sound. The English translation by the present author of the part of the story after King Bimbisāra's death (*T* 1450: 191a19–b26) is in the appendix.

The differences between the illustrations of the child drummer and the adult drummer are manifold. The illustrations of an adult drummer are more numerous than that of the child. They are found in Kizil Cave 80 (**Fig. 3**),[12] Kizil Cave 101 (**Fig. 4**),[13] Kizil Cave 104,[14] Kizil Cave 184,[15] Kizil Cave 186 (**Fig. 5**),[16] Kizil Cave

11 Simsim Cave 30, main chamber, barrel vault, left haunch, register and number unclear, *in situ*. Illustrated in *ZXBY* 2009: V, 19, pl. 17.

12 Kizil Cave 80 (Höllentopfhöhle), main chamber, barrel vault, right haunch, 6th register, no. 5, *in situ*. Illustrated on a historical photograph taken on the third German expedition in 1906, kept in the Museum für Asiatische Kunst, Berlin, no. B 620; in Tan/An 1981: I, pl. 180; *Kizil Grottoes* 1983–1985/1989–1997: II, pl. 53; visible in *ZXBY* 2009: II, 253, pl. 225.

13 Kizil Cave 101, main chamber, barrel vault, left haunch, 4th register, no. 4, *in situ*. Illustrated in Tan/An 1981: I, pl. 201; *Kizil Grottoes* 1983–1985/1989–1997: II, pl. 94; *ZXBQ* 2008: 144, pl. 127; *ZXBY* 2009: III, 64, pl. 54.

14 Kizil Cave 104, main chamber, barrel vault, left haunch, 6th register, no. 2, *in situ*. Illustrated in *Kizil Grottoes* 1983–1985/1989–1997: II, pl. 99.

15 Kizil Cave 184 (Drittletzte Höhle, 2. Schlucht), main chamber, front lunette. The mural was exhibited in the former Museum für Völkerkunde in Berlin (no. IB 8446) and was lost during the Second World War.

16 There are two examples of this image in Kizil Cave 186 (Mittlere Höhle, 2. Schlucht). The first image is found on the front lunette of the main chamber. As the exact location of this image is not known, it is not sure whether this image of the adult drum-

224,[17] Kizilgaha Cave 11,[18] Simsim Cave 1,[19] and Simsim Cave 36.[20] The adult drummer is bare from the waist up while wearing a scarf in most of the examples, except in the representation in Kizilgaha Cave 11, where his upper body is possibly clothed with animal skin. He wears long pants in all of the above examples, whereas the boy drummer is naked and often wears ornaments. A historical photograph of the barrel vault ceiling in Kizil Cave 80 shows the drummer seated while playing the drum with both hands (**Fig. 3**). As in Kizil Cave 80, most of the examples of adult drummer show him as seated while playing the drum. In the examples from Kizil Cave 101 (**Fig. 4**) and Kizil Cave 244 the adult drummer beats the drum while standing. In these images, one can even see the strings tied to the heads of the drum on both sides. The adult drummer plays the drum with his hands, whereas the child drummer plays with a drum stick. The child drummer appears to play a cylindrical or barrel drum, but the adult drummer always plays an hourglass drum, except in the representation in Kizil Cave 186 (**Fig. 5**), where he seems to play a barrel drum. In Kizil Caves 184 and 186, there are the depictions of the child drummer on the rear lunette and the adult drummer on the front lunette of the main chamber. In Kizil Cave 186, there is also an additional example of the adult drummer on the right haunch of the barrel vault in the main chamber. It implies that the monastics who commissioned the painting of these two caves knew both stories.

Fig. 3 Adult drummer and Buddha. Kizil Cave 80 (Höllentopfhöhle), main chamber, barrel vault, right haunch, 6th register, no. 5, in situ. The drummer illustration is at the third line from the bottom, next to the right side end. Historical photograph taken on the third German expedition in 1906, no. B 620 © Staatliche Museen zu Berlin, Museum für Asiatische Kunst

Turning to the subject of drums in the paintings, they tell us much about the specifics of musical performance at Kucha. It is difficult to say that the drums in the paintings were exact copies of the drums circulated in Kucha, as the painters could have used other sources such as earlier paintings rather than a real drum for their model. Nevertheless, these drums in the paintings look very simi-

mer is on the direct opposite of the child drummer illustration on the rear lunette of this cave. Illustrated in *ZXBY* 2009: III, 147, pl. 128. The second image is on the main chamber, barrel vault, right haunch, probably 3rd register, no. 4, *in situ*. Illustrated in TAN/AN 1981: II, pl. 117; *Kizil Grottoes* 1983–1985/1989–1997: III, pl. 51; *ZXBQ* 2008: 173, pl. 154.

17 Kizil Cave 224, main chamber, barrel vault, right haunch, 5th register, no. 8, *in situ*. Illustrated in TAN/AN 1981: II, pl. 188; *Kizil Grottoes* 1983–1985/1989–1997: III, pl. 151; *ZXBY* 2009: II, 163, pl. 145.

18 Kizilgaha Cave 11, main chamber, barrel vault, left haunch, 2nd register, number unclear, *in situ*.

19 Simsim Cave 1, main chamber, barrel vault, left haunch, 2nd register, no. 1, *in situ*.

20 Simsim Cave 36, main chamber, barrel vault, left haunch, probably 2nd register, *in situ*.

Fig. 4 Adult drummer and Buddha. Kizil Cave 101, main chamber, barrel vault, left haunch, 4th register, no. 4, in situ. After TAN/AN *1981: I, pl. 201*

Fig. 5 Adult drummer and Buddha with an attendant monk. Kizil Cave 186 (Mittlere Höhle, 2. Schlucht), main chamber, barrel vault, right haunch, probably 3rd register, no. 4, in situ. After TAN/AN *1981: II, pl. 117*

lar to the musical instruments supposedly played in the Kuchean music, as the composition of dancers and musicians needed to play the music is described in the *Old Book of Tang* completed in 945 CE.[21] The drum held by the child drummer is a small barrel drum with two faces, seemingly close to the *dalagu* drum that ZHENG has identified in the Dunhuang murals.[22] According to THRASHER, this *dalagu* drum was played with the hands and possibly linked with the Persian drum *dholak*.[23] In the paintings of Kucha, however, the boys often play the drum with a stick. Despite the difference in playing method, its shape and size suggest that it is closest to the *dalagu* drum. The drum played by the adult drummer is similar to the *paṇava* drum in the *stūpa* relief from Nalanda II ruin from the 6th and 7th centuries CE.[24] The *paṇava* drum was a rhythm instrument in the orchestra of the theatre piece mentioned in the *Nāṭyaśāstra*,[25] which the drummer put under his left arm, controlling the pitch by tightening and loosening his grip on the strings, hitting it with his right hand or a stick.[26] The *tantrīpaṭahika* described in the *Harṣacarita* translated by COWELL and THOMAS as the "string drum" used for playing background music for the female dancers might also be related to the drum played by the adult drummer in the picture.[27] The drum also looks similar to the "slender waist drum" *xiyaogu* or *zhanggu* mentioned in the Chinese annals regarding the music of Kucha.[28] The "slender waist drum" has drumheads on both sides of an hourglass-shaped shell, with the drumheads fastened by

21 *Old Book of Tang*: XXIX "Yinyue er/Music 2", "Qiuci yue / Music of Kucha".
22 ZHENG 2007: 90.
23 THRASHER 2015.
24 KAUFMANN 1986: 176.
25 DICK 2016.
26 *Ibid.*
27 ZIN 2004: 340. *Harṣacarita*: 131; English translation: COWELL/THOMAS 1897: 113.
28 OH 1996: 288, table 13.

cords to enable fastening and loosening. Drummers could play the instrument with their hands or a drum stick.

Interestingly, this drum has survived in Korean traditional music with its original name in Korean pronunciation, *janggu*,[29] although it is unsure whether the form of the drum has stayed exactly the same. Based on the Dunhuang murals painted during the Tang dynasty (618–917 CE), one can conclude that there were indeed slender waist drums in Western China.[30] There is a porcelain replica of the *xiyaogu*, 58.9 cm wide with a drum face diameter of 22.2 cm, dating from the Tang dynasty and found at the Lushan kiln site, Henan Province, which is now in the Palace Museum, Beijing. Described as a "speckle-glazed waist drum", it has a similar shape to the *xiyaogu* drums in the paintings from Kucha and Dunhuang.[31]

Finally, turning to the specific combination of performed music and musical offering at Kucha, it is worth repeating SASAKI's observation that although the Buddha had prohibited monks and nuns from performing music or theatre, laypeople could offer music to the Buddha.[32] In the later development of the *vinaya*, monks and nuns may enjoy the performance as spectators if it is an offering to the Buddha.[33] There is a record numbered Cp. 7 from the monastery site in Duldur-Akhur that the monastics also "bought alcoholic beverage for the musicians", showing that Kuchean Buddhists would have enjoyed the music at the monastery and paid the musicians with the liquor.[34] Furthermore, the sound of the drum could be an offering worthy of a promised future life as a Buddha. This idea seems to have also been transmitted in Tibetan Buddhism. In the *Bhadrakalpikasūtra*, the Buddhas Sāgara and Sukrama were musicians in their past lives and played the drum for contemporary Buddhas.[35] Not only musicians, but a former sweeper, the Buddha Priyacakṣurvaktra, also beat the drum in homage to the Buddha and obtained the prophecy of his future Buddhahood.[36]

The representations of the child and adult drummers are fascinating examples that show traces of Kucha's music and religion. The stories of drummers surviving in the collection of monastic rules for the Mūlasarvāstivāda school and their illustrations in Kucha's Buddhist caves imply that these caves were possibly linked to that school of Buddhism. Moreover, it seems that the Kucheans pursued to convey the music visually for everyone visiting the cave to see. The drums in the paintings are similar in their shapes to the real, local drums. Their images alluded to the real percussion music possibly played in the region, still making their sounds in the viewers' imaginations.

29 THRASHER 2015.
30 ZHENG 2007: 88–95.
31 The image can be accessed via the Palace Museum website: (Chinese) https://www.dpm.org.cn/collection/ceramic/226730.html (accessed April 2022); (English) https://en.dpm.org.cn/collections/collections/2009-10-16/707.html (accessed April 2022).
32 SASAKI 1991: 1–2.
33 SASAKI 1991: 16–21.
34 CHING 2017: 234.
35 SKILLING/SAERJI 2016: 171; SKILLING/SAERJI 2017: 188.
36 SKILLING/SAERJI 2017: 203.

BIBLIOGRAPHY

Harṣacarita = *The Harṣacharita of Bāṇabhaṭṭa with the commentary Sanketa of Śankarakavi*, eds. Kasinath Pandurang Parab & Nārāyana Rāma Ācārya, Bombay, 1946; transl. COWELL/THOMAS 1897.

Old Book of Tang = *Jiu Tang shu* 舊唐書 (compiled by Liu Xu 劉昫, 946 CE). https://ctext.org/wiki.pl?if=gb&res=456206 [accessed April 2022].

T = *Taishō Shinshū Daizōkyō* 大正新脩大藏經, eds. Junjirō Takakusu 高楠順次郎, Kaigyoku Watanabe 渡辺海旭 & Genmyō Ono 小野玄妙. 100 vols. Tokyo, 1924–1934.

* * *

BEAL, Samuel, transl. (1884) *Si-yu-ki: Buddhist Records of the Western World. Translated from the Chinese of Hiuen Tsiang (A. D. 629)*. 2 vols. London.

CHING, Chao-Jung 庆昭蓉 (2017) *Tuhuoluoyu shisu wenxian yu gudai Qiuci lishi* 吐火罗语世俗文献与古代龟兹历史 / *Tocharian Secular Texts and History of Ancient Kucha*. Beijing (Weiming Zhongguoshi congkan. Di 9 zhong).

COWELL, Edward Byles & Frederick Williams THOMAS, transl. (1897) *The Harṣacarita of Bāṇa*. London.

DICK, Alastair (2016) *Paṇavas. Grove Music Online*. https://doi.org/10.1093/gmo/9781561592630.article.L2291318 [accessed April 2022].

KAUFMANN, Walter (1981) *Altindien*. Leipzig (Musikgeschichte in Bildern: Bd. 2, Lfg. 8).

Kizil Grottoes 1983–1985 = *Chūgoku sekkutsu: Kijiru sekkutsu* 中国石窟: キジル石窟 / *The Grotto Art of China: The Kizil Grottoes*, eds. Shinkyō Uiguru jichiku bunbutsu kanri iinkai 新疆ウイグル自治区文物

管理委員会 & Haijō ken Kijiru senbutsudō bunbutsu hokanjo 拜城県キジル千仏洞文物保管所 (1983–1985). 3 vols. Tokyo.

Kizil Grottoes 1989–1997 = *Zhongguo shiku: Kezi'er shiku* 中国石窟: 克孜尔石窟 [The Grotto Art of China: The Kizil Grottoes], eds. Xinjiang Weiwu'er zizhiqu wenwu guanli weiyuanhui 新疆维吾尔自治区文物管理委员会 & Baicheng xian Kezi'er qianfodong wenwu baoguansuo 拜城县克孜尔千佛洞文物保管所 (1989–1997). 3 vols. Beijing.

MA, Shichang 馬世長 (1984) Kijiru sekkutsu chūshinchūku no shūshitsu kucchō to kōshitsu no hekiga キジル石窟中心柱窟の主室窟頂と後室の壁画 / Paintings on Main Chamber's Barrel Vault and Wall of Back Corridor, in Square Columned Caves at the Kizil Grottoes. In: *Kizil Grottoes* 1983–1985: II, 170–236.

——(1996) Kezi'er zhongxinzhuku zhushi xuanding yu houshi de bihua 克孜尔中心柱窟主室券顶与后室的壁画 [Paintings on Main Chamber's Barrel Vault and Wall of Back Corridor, in Square Columned Caves at the Kizil Grottoes]. In: *Kizil Grottoes* 1989–1997: II, 174–226.

MA, Qin 马秦 & Shucai FAN 范书财, eds. (2007) *Qiuci: Zaoxiang* 龟兹: 造像 [Figural Images in Kucha]. Beijing.

OBERLIES, Thomas (2003) Ein bibliographischer Überblick über die kanonischen Texte der Śrāvakayāna-Schulen des Buddhismus (ausgenommen der des Mahāvihāra-Theravāda). *Wiener Zeitschrift für die Kunde Südasiens / Vienna Journal of South Asian Studies* (Vienna) 47: 37–84.

OGIHARA, Hirotoshi 荻原裕敏 (2011) Notes on Some Tocharian Vinaya Fragments in the London and Paris Collections. *Tocharian and Indo-European Studies* (Copenhagen) 12: 111–144.

——(2012) Tokarago B no Avadāna shahon danpen ni tsuite トカラ語 Bの『Avadāna 写本』断片について / The "Avadāna manuscript" in Tocharian B. *Tōkyō daigaku gengo-gaku ronshū* 東京大学言語学論集 / *Tokyo University Linguistics Papers* (Tokyo) 32: 109–243.

——(2013) Notes on Some Tocharian Vinaya Fragments in the Paris Collection. *Tocharian and Indo-European Studies* (Copenhagen) 14: 187–211.

OH, Cheoul Hwan [O, Ch'ŏlhwan] 오철환 (1996) Kodae K'uch'a ŭmak ko 고대 쿠차(龜玆) 음악고 / A Study on the Kucha Music. *Chungang Asia yŏn'gu* 중앙아시아연구 / *Central Asian Studies* (Seoul) 1: 273–298, 373–374.

PANGLUNG, Jampa Losang (1981) *Die Erzählstoffe des Mūlasarvāstivāda-Vinaya, analysiert auf Grund der tibetischen Übersetzung*. Tokyo (Studia philologica Buddhica / Monograph series 3).

ROSEN, Valentina (1959) *Der Vinayavibhaṅga zum Bhikṣuprātimokṣa der Sarvāstivādins: Sanskritfragmente nebst e. Analyse d. chines. Übersetzung*. Berlin (Institut für Orientforschung: Veröffentlichung 27; Sanskrittexte aus den Turfanfunden 2).

ROTMAN, Andy (2008) *Divine Stories. Divyāvadāna*. Part I. Boston.

SASAKI, Shizuka 佐々木 閑 (1991) Biku to gigaku 比丘と伎楽 / Monastic Worship of Stūpas with Music and Dance in Vinaya Texts. *Bukkyō shigaku kenkyū* 佛教史學研究 / *Journal of the History of the Buddhism* (Kyoto) 34.1: 1–24.

SKILLING, Peter & SAERJI (2016) How the Buddhas of the Fortunate Aeon First Aspired to Awakening: The *pūrva-praṇidhāna*s of Buddhas 251–500. *Annual Report of the International Research Institute for Advanced Buddhology at Soka University for the Academic Year* 2015 (Tokyo) 19: 149–192.

SKILLING, Peter & SAERJI (2017) How the Buddhas of the Fortunate Aeon First Aspired to Awakening: The *pūrva-praṇidhāna*s of Buddhas 501–750. *Annual Report of the International Research Institute for Advanced Buddhology at Soka University for the Academic Year* 2016 (Tokyo) 20: 167–204.

TAN, SHUTONG 譚樹桐 & Chunyang AN 安春陽 (1981) *Shinkyō no hekiga: Kijiru senbutsudō* 新疆の壁画: キジル千仏洞 / *Murals for Xinjiang: the Thousand-Buddha Caves at Kizil*. Kyōto / Beijing.

THRASHER, Alan R. (2015) *Xiyaogu. Grove Music Online*. https://doi.org/10.1093/gmo/9781561592630.article.L2281930 [accessed March 2022].

ZHENG, Ruzhong 郑汝中, ed. (2007) *Foguo de tianlai zhi yin* 佛国的天籁之音 [Heavenly Sounds of the Buddha World]. Shanghai.

ZIN, Monika (2004) Die altindischen *vīṇā*s. *Studien zur Musikarchäologie IV*, eds. E. Hickmann & R. Eichmann. Rahden (Orient-Archäologie 15): 321–362.

ZXBQ 2008 = *Zhongguo Xinjiang bihua: Qiuci* 中国新疆壁画: 龟兹 / *Mural Paintings in Xinjiang of China: Qiuci* [Kucha], ed. Xinjiang Qiuci shiku yanjiusuo 新疆龟兹石窟研究所. Urumqi, 2008.

ZXBY 2009 =*Zhongguo Xinjiang bihua yishu* 中国新疆壁画艺术 [Compendium of Murals in Xinjiang, China], ed. *Zhongguo Xinjiang bihua yishu bianji weiyuanhui* 中国新疆壁画艺术编辑委员会. 6 vols. Urumqi, 2009.

Appendix: English Translations of the Stories of a Drummer in *T* 1442 and *T* 1450 by Ji Ho Yi

(The names of the heavens and hells mentioned in the translations are mainly based on "The Cosmos According to the *Divyāvadāna*" in ROTMAN 2008: 377–379.)

Story of the Child Drummer in the *Mūlasarvāstivāda-vinaya*, *T* 1442: 835a13–c9.

At the time, the Buddha readily took the straight road and arrived at a village. Then there were two little boys playing at the village gate. One held a drum; the other held a bow. When the two boys saw the Buddha coming, they immediately and readily honoured the Buddha's feet and said to him, "Bhagavat, welcome! Welcome! Why would the Bhagavat want to follow a dangerous road to walk around? We only want the Bhagavat not to have fear. We will be the guides for the Bhagavat." One boy went ahead, beating the drum. The other held a bow and an arrow and came following [the group] at the back. The Buddha saw them off and immediately thought, "These two boys planted the good root long ago, [and] now met me." [The Buddha] told them, "You, two boys, can now return and go. The great teacher Bhagavat has long been freed of fear. What could lions, tigers, and leopards do?" One boy sounded the drum in front of the Buddha, and the other faced the Buddha and plucked the bow. They honoured the feet [of the Buddha] and finally returned to their original place. Then the Buddha immediately expressed a smile. Various lights were flowing out of his mouth, so-called blue, yellow, red, and white, the colour of vermilion crystal (Skt. *spaṭikā*, Chin. *pazhi* 頗胝). Some of this bright light descended, and some, again, ascended. The light that sank below to the Reviving Hell (Skt. *sañjīva*, Chin. *suhuodiyu* 速活地獄), Black Thread Hell (Skt. *kālasūtra*, Chin. *heisheng* 黑繩), Hell of Group Assembly (Chin. *zhonghe* 眾合),[37] Shrieking Hell (Skt. *raurava*, Chin. *xiaojiao* 小叫), Loud Shrieking hell (Skt. *mahāraurava*, Chin. *dajiao* 大叫), Hell of Heat (Skt. *tapana*, Chin. *xiaore* 小熱), Hell of Extreme Heat (Skt. *pratāpana*, Chin. *dare* 大熱), Hell of Ceaseless Torture (Skt. *avīci*, Chin. *apidiyu* 阿毘地獄) and eight Cold Hells. The lights arrived there, and it was as if all the sentient beings receiving blazing heat received coolness, and [the beings] in the ice suddenly caught warmth. All those sentient beings were freed from pain and felt comfort and joy, [and] said this phrase: "I and you all, did we die at hell and be born somewhere else?" As the Buddha wanted those sentient beings to arouse faith and joy, he immediately sent his [magically conjured] transformation bodies, and all [of them] said this phrase: "We did not die here and [be] given rebirth somewhere else. This [unusual event] must be due to the virtuous powers of the rare, mysterious, great man, making our bodies and souls free of pain and gaining happiness."

Conceiving the faith and suddenly eliminating all pains of hell, [those sentient beings were reborn] as sorts of humans and gods (*deva*) receiving magnificent, mysterious bodies, always being the vessels of *dharma* and able to see the truth. The [lights] that went above reached the Heaven of Four Great Kings (Skt. *cāturmahārājika*, Chin. *sidawangzhongtian* 四大王眾天), Heaven of the Thirty-Three (Skt. *trāyastriṃśa*, Chin. *sanshisantian* 三十三天), Heaven of the Yama (Chin. *yemotian* 夜摩天), Tuṣita heaven (Chin. *dushiduotian* 覩史多天), Delighting in Creation Heaven (Skt. *nirmāṇarati*, Chin. *hualetian* 化樂天), Masters of Others' Creations Heaven (Skt. *paranirmitavaśavartin*, Chin. *tahuazizaitian* 他化自在天), Heaven of Brahmā's Assembly (Skt. *brahmakāyika*, Chin. *fanzhong* 梵眾), Heaven of Brahmā's Priests (Skt. *brahmapurohita*, Chin. *fanfu* 梵輔), Great Brahmā Heaven (Skt. *mahābrahmaṇa*, Chin. *dafan* 大梵), Heaven of Limited Splendour (Skt. *parīttābha*, Chin. *shaoguang* 少光), Heaven of Immeasurable Splendour (Skt. *apramāṇābha*, Chin. *wuliangguang* 無量光), Radiant Heaven (Skt. *ābhāsvara*, Chin. *guangyin* 光音), Heaven of Limited Beauty (Skt. *parīttaśubha*, Chin. *shaojing* 少淨), Heaven of Immeasurable Beauty (Skt. *apramāṇaśubha*, Chin. *wuliangjing* 無量淨), Heaven of Complete Beauty (Skt. *śubhakṛtsna*, Chin. *bianjing* 遍淨), Unclouded Heaven (Skt. *anabhraka*, Chin. *wuyun* 無雲), Heaven of Merit Born (Skt. *puṇyaprasava*, Chin. *fusheng* 福生), Heaven of Great Result (Skt. *bṛhatphala*, Chin. *guangguo* 廣果), Heaven of No Affliction (Skt. *abṛha*, Chin. *wufan*

37 *T* 1442, ed. vol. 23: 835a25; ROTMAN 2008: 378. This seems to be the equivalent of the Crushing Hell written in Sanskrit as *saṅghāta*, but the translator possibly understood Sanskrit as *saṃgata* meaning the group assembly and translated the word as *zhonghe* 眾合.

無煩),[38] Serene Heaven (Skt. *atapa*, Chin. *wure* 無熱), Good-Looking Heaven (Skt. *sudṛśa*, Chin. *shanjian* 善見), Clear-Sighted Heaven (Skt. *sudarśa*, Chin. *shanjian* 善現), Supreme Heaven (Skt. *akaniṣṭha*, Chin. *sejiujingtian* 色究竟天). Where the light was shed, the sermon was given among the light, about the pain, the emptiness, the impermanence, the non-self. Moreover, these two verses were sung: "You should seek renunciation, vigorously strive to follow the Buddha's teaching, defeat the soldiers of life and death, like an elephant destroying a grass hut. In this precept, always practice and do not idle, [you] can dry the sea of affliction, [you] should eliminate the pain to its boundaries." Then that bright light shone upon the three thousand great thousand worlds (billion worlds) and returned to the Buddha's place. When the Buddha would preach about past events, the light went into his back. When he would talk about the future, the light went into his chest. When explaining about hells, the light went into his soles. When talking about the deeds of non-human animals, the light went into his heels. When talking about *preta*s, the light went into his toes. When preaching about human matters, the light went into his knees. When talking about the powerful-wheel king (Skt. *balacakravartin*, Chin. *lilunwang* 力輪王), the light went into the palm of his left hand. When preaching about the wheel-turning king (Skt. *cakravartin*, Chin. *zhuanlunwang* 轉輪王), the light went into his right palm. When talking about gods (*deva*), the light went into his navel. When talking about the *śrāvaka*s, the light went into his mouth. When talking about the *pratyekabuddha*s, the light went between his eyebrows. When talking about perfectly enlightened Buddhas, the light went into his *uṣṇīṣa*. The bright light circled the Buddha three times and went into his *uṣṇīṣa* this time.

The elder Ānanda put his hands together and respectfully said to the Buddha, "Bhagavat, Tathāgata, Arhat, the Buddha would not joyfully smile without a cause." Then [he] sung a verse. "The Bhagavat has long abandoned the arrogance. Among the sentient beings [he is] the highest. [Having] conquered the afflictions and all hatred, [he] would not smile without a cause. The Tathāgata would himself prove the true mysterious enlightenment; all those who can hear will be delighted. The *muni* greatest victorious would like to preach. The crowd's doubtful hearts will be open wide." The Buddha told Ānanda, "Yes! Yes! The Tathāgata, the Arhat, the Buddha, does not manifest a smile without a cause. Did you see the two young boys guiding us or not?" [Ānanda] answered the Buddha, "I saw." The Buddha told Ānanda, "Due to this good root, within the future thirteen *kalpa*s, [they] will not fall into unfortunate rebirths and be born among people and gods (*deva*). Their last bodies would fulfil perfect enlightenment (Skt. *anuttarā-samyak-saṃbodhi*, Chin. *wushang zhengdeng puti* 無上正等菩提). One will be named Dharma-drum-sound-Tathāgata (Chin. *Faguyin rulai* 法鼓音如來), and the other will be named Bestowing-fearlessness-Tathāgata (Chin. *Shiwuwei rulai* 施無畏如來)." Then the Buddha preached this revelation and followed the road and left, arrived at a village amid the corner of the forest and lodged.

The other version in *T* 1443 (984b01–985a6) is only different in that the two boys are not guides, but they come in front of the Buddha to play music for him, sounding a drum and plucking the bow.

Story of the Adult Drummer in the *Mūlasarvāstivāda-vinaya, Saṅghabhedavastu*, *T* 1450: 191a19–b26.

At the time, all ministers came and told the Great King, "The Old King [Bimbisāra]'s body has now perished." Hearing these words, [the King Ajātaśatru] fell to the ground in despair. Then by splashing water on the face, [the King Ajātaśatru] came back to his senses and woke, immediately went into the room, [and] wore the mourning dress for his father. No one could advise him and free him of his grief. Then the ministers all discussed, "Which methods could free our king from grief?" At the time, a musician from South India came [to the country], [the ministers] invited him to the king's residence to play all sorts of music. The king's heart felt no joy. [The king] was silent and would not answer, and he did not give [the musician] any compliment. The musician left, [then] travelled and arrived at the Buddha's place [and] said, "Good. Sir!" The heart rejoiced and immediately beat the drum and made music. At the time, the Buddha himself immediately emitted the light and smiled. Various kinds of light were emitted, and [it] was like Mars, that light went above and below. The light went below and reached the Avīci hell. Where the light shone, one suffering from coldness became warm immediately. One suffering from heat felt coolness. All those suffering

38 *T* 1442, ed. vol. 23: 835b9; ROTMAN 2008: 378. The translation of *wufan* 無煩 or *abṛha* as "Heaven of No Affliction", based on the Chinese word *wufan*, deviates from ROTMAN's translation as "Not Great".

gained rest. They all thought, "I achieved the rebirth elsewhere." The Buddha conjured a person in hell and said [to them], "You are not reborn elsewhere. There was someone else who shone bright light and put suffering to rest." All sinners saw that conjured person, their hearts rejoiced, their sins disappeared, and all gained rebirth among people and gods (*deva*), receiving and hearing the four sacred precepts. The light went above and reached the Heaven of Four Great Kings (Skt. *cāturmahārājika*, Chin. *sitianwang* 四天王), Heaven of the Thirty-Three (Skt. *trāyastriṃśa*, Chin. *sanshisantian* 三十三天), up to the Supreme Heaven (Skt. *akaniṣṭha*, Chin. *ajianizhatian* 阿迦尼吒天), among the light, [the Buddha] preached the impermanence, pain, a eulogy on the emptiness of the *dharma*. That light shone throughout the three thousand, great thousand worlds (billion worlds) and returned to the Buddha, following after him. If [the Buddha would preach about] the Buddhas or the perfect enlightenment, when he would preach about the past events, the light gathered and went into his back. When talking about future events, the light went into his front. When preaching about hell, the light went into his soles. When wanting to talk about the non-human animals, the light went into the back of his heels. When talking about *preta*s, the light went into his toes. When preaching about humans, the light went into his shins. Preaching about the wheel-turning king (Skt. *cakravartin*, Chin. *zhuanlunwangzhe* 轉輪王者), the light would be extinguished in the middle of his left palm. When talking about the great wheel-turning king (Skt. *mahācakravartin*, Chin. *dazhuanlunwangzhe* 大轉輪王者), the light went into his right hand and [was] extinguished there. When talking about the gods (*deva*), the light went into his navel. When talking about *śrāvaka*s or *pratyekabuddha*s, the light went into his arms. When talking about the *dharma*s of *pratyekabuddha*s, the light went between his eyebrows. When talking about the *dharma*s of perfect enlightenment, the light went into his *uṣṇīṣa*. Broadly it is the same as what was discussed before.[39] When the bright light arrived at the Buddha's place, it circled the Buddha three times and went between his eyebrows.

Then Ānanda collected his hands and praised the Buddha in verses, broadly the same as discussed before.[40] [He] praised the Buddha with verses. "Thousand various mysterious sorts of colours are emitted from the mouth in a flow. Broadly shone upon the ten directions, it is also like the sunrise. Selfless, preaching in verses, [the Buddha] eliminates the arrogance of the listeners. All causes of becoming a Buddha, the light will not shine without a cause, conquering hatred and the like." The Buddha asked Ānanda, "Did you see or not see that musician delighting at me beating the drum and making music?" Ānanda answered the Buddha, "I did see." The Buddha told Ānanda again, "That musician will be a *pratyekabuddha*, named Gracious-harmonious-sound (Chin. *Yaheyin* 雅和音)."

Deutsche Zusammenfassung

Die buddhistischen Höhlen der antiken Kucha-Region enthalten in ihren Tonnengewölben erzählende Malereien mit Trommlern. Es gibt zwei Arten von Bildern. Der erste Typus zeigt ein Kind, das eine große Trommel schlägt. Der zweite Typus stellt eine erwachsene männliche Person dar, die eine sanduhrförmige Hüfttrommel schlägt. Während die Bilder zwei Geschichten aus dem *vinaya* der Mūlasarvāstivādins zu illustrieren scheinen, die im Anhang ins Englische übersetzt sind, spiegeln die Trommeln auf den Gemälden echte Trommeln wider, die in ihrer Form den Trommeln aus Persien und Indien ähneln und, wie im *Alten Buch von Tang* beschrieben, in Kucha bekannt waren. Bild und Text zusammen zeigen die Idee, dass der Trommelschlag auch eine Opfergabe für den Buddha sein konnte.

39 *T* 1450, ed. vol. 24: 191b16 "廣如前說". The preceding sentence is Yijing's comment.

40 *T* 1450, ed. vol. 24: 191b18 "廣說如前". The preceding sentence is a comment by Yijing.

Die Konservierung und Restaurierung von Wandmalereien aus der Studiensammlung des Museums für Asiatische Kunst, Berlin

Marie Fortmann, Angela Mitschke, Joana Schaer

Der Umzug des Museums für Asiatische Kunst in das neu errichtete Humboldt Forum in Berlin erlaubte eine Erweiterung der Ausstellung. Somit entstand die Möglichkeit, mehrere Jahrzehnte in der Studiensammlung des Museums verwahrte, herausragende Kunstwerke wieder der Öffentlichkeit zu präsentieren. Unter anderem sollten fünf Wandmalereikomplexe mit buddhistischen Darstellungen einen neuen Platz in der Dauerausstellung erhalten. Die Wandmalereien, entstanden im 6. bis 7. Jahrhundert, wurden 1913–1914 im Zuge der 4. sogenannten Preußischen Turfan-Expeditionen[1] von Höhlenwänden abgenommen und nach Berlin transportiert. Die folgenden Jahrzehnte hinterließen Spuren an den 43 Malereiplatten. Vorbereitungen für frühere Ausstellungen, Kriegsschäden und damit einhergehende Restaurierungen waren an den Kunstwerken abzulesen. Eine Konservierung und Restaurierung der Malereien vor einer erneuten Präsentation erwiesen sich als unerlässlich. Grundlage der Arbeiten waren die Untersuchung des Bestandes und Zustandes, Schadensursachenforschungen und Kartierungen. Resultierend aus den gewonnenen Ergebnissen konnten Testreihen angelegt und ein Konzept zur Konservierung, Restaurierung und Präsentation der wertvollen Malereien erarbeitet werden. Die Umsetzung der konzipierten Maßnahmen wurde im Team von vier Diplom-Restauratorinnen[2] ausgeführt und durch die Kuratorin für Zentralasiatische Kunst Frau Dr. Lilla Russell-Smith und den Chefrestaurator des Hauses Toralf Gabsch M.A. fachlich begleitet.

Die bearbeiteten Wandmalereien stammen aus drei verschiedenen Höhlen in Kizil,[3] einem buddhistischen Höhlenkomplex am westlichen Abschnitt der nördlich um die Taklamakanwüste verlaufenden Route der antiken Seidenstraße im heutigen Xinjiang (VR China). Auch wenn der Aufbau der Malereien ähnlich ist, so gibt es dennoch Unterschiede. Den Malschichtträger bilden mit Stroh armierte Lehmputze, wobei die Lehmfarbigkeit zwischen graugrün und rotbraun variiert, was vermutlich auf einen unterschiedlichen Eisenanteil im Lehm zurückzuführen ist. Über einer dünnen Grundierung erfolgte der Auftrag der Malerei in Seccotechnik mit einem Temperabindemittel. Häufig ist ein mehrschichtiger Farbauftrag erkennbar (**Abb. 1**). Die vielfältigen Darstellungen der bearbeiteten Szenen reichen von filigranen, figürlichen Malereien höchster künstlerischer Qualität bis hin zu einfacheren Rautenmustern.

Die Abnahme und der Transport bedingten die Teilung der fünf Malereikomplexe von insgesamt 20 Quadratmetern in zunächst 43 händelbare Einzelstücke. Nach der Ankunft in Berlin erfolgte die Restaurierung der Malereien. Hierbei wurden die Fragmente sortiert und auf einen Hilfsträger aufgebracht. Theodor Bartus, der mehr als 50 Jahre als Museumstechniker und Konservator am damaligen Museum für Völkerkunde tätig war, hat sich neben seiner Teilnahme an den Expeditionen intensiv um die Restaurierung der mitgebrachten Exponate verdient gemacht. So war er für die Konservierung, Aufstellung

1 Als Turfan-Expeditionen werden vier Expeditionen des Berliner Völkerkundemuseums bezeichnet, die in den Jahren 1902–1914 den nördlich des Tarimbeckens verlaufenden Teil der antiken Seidenstraße im heutigen Xinjiang (VR China) bereisten und nach ihrem ersten Erkundungsort Turfan benannt wurden. Die Expeditionen dienten der Erfassung und Erforschung von Kunst- und Kulturschätzen in einst buddhistischen Tempelanlagen.

2 Dipl. Rest. Marie Fortmann (ehem. Heyer), Dipl. Rest. Angela Mitschke, Dipl. Rest. Susan Nitsche und Dipl. Rest. Joana Schaer.

3 Höhle 13, Inv.-Nr. III 8860, III 8859a, III 8859b; Höhle 179 (Japanerhöhle), Inv.-Nr. III 8660; Höhle 219 (Ajātaśatru-Höhle), Inv.-Nr. III 8881.

Abb. 1 Kizil, Höhle 179 (Japanerhöhle), Predigender Buddha, Inv.-Nr. III 8660, Detail, Malerei – filigrane, figürliche Darstellungen, mehrschichtiger Farbauftrag © S. Nitsche, 2017

und Instandhaltung der Turfan-Funde zuständig. Zur dauerhaften Sicherung und Präsentation der abgenommenen Malereien wurden sie in einem flächigen, mehrere Zentimeter starken Gipsbett gesichert und entsprechend der damaligen Standards restauriert.[4] Historische Aufnahmen belegen, dass einige der Malereien im Museum für Völkerkunde ausgestellt waren. In den folgenden Jahrzehnten prägten kriegsbedingte Schäden und erneute Restaurierungen den überkommenen Zustand der Kunstwerke.

Der folgende Abschnitt widmet sich der aktuellen Konservierung und Restaurierung der herausragenden Wandmalereien am Beispiel einer der fünf bearbeiteten Szenen. Die von dem Archäologen, Indologen und einem der Organisatoren der deutschen Turfan-Expeditionen, Albert Grünwedel (1856–1935), als Ajātaśatru-Höhle bezeichnete Höhle ist die erste in der zweiten Anlage von Kizil (Höhle 219). GRÜNWEDEL berichtet in seinen Aufzeichnungen, dass die Höhle den bekannten Typus aufweist: eine Cella mit einem Pfeiler als Rückwand, rechts

Abb. 2 Kizil, Höhle 219 (Ajātaśatru-Höhle), Arhat mit Flammen, Inv.-Nr. III 8881, Detail, Vorzustand © S. Nitsche, 2017

4 Vgl. VAN TANGERLOO/KNÜPPEL/GABSCH 2012: 31.

und links davon schmale Gänge, die mit einem breiten Quergang am hinteren Ende verbunden sind und so um den Pfeiler herumführen. Die abgenommene Wandmalerei entstammt der Rückseite des Pfeilers im hinteren Gang (**Abb. 2, 3**).[5] Grünwedel beschreibt die Malerei folgendermaßen: „In der Nische gegenüber dem Nirvana waren zwei meditierende Arhats dargestellt mit Flammen hinter den Schultern. [...] Über diesen Arhats lief ein gemalter Balkon hin mit einer äußerst pathetisch klagenden Königsfamilie, ähnlich der Verwandten in der entspr. Höhle 3. Anl., doch nicht so gut erhalten wie dort."[6] Auffällig ist, dass die Darstellung der klagenden Königs- oder Fürstenfamilie in anderen Fällen meist oberhalb einer Malerei, welche die Verbrennung der Leiche des Buddha zeigt, positioniert ist. Eventuell befand sich in der Nische die Skulptur eines Mönches im Zusammenhang mit der umgebenen Wandmalerei.[7]

Abb. 3 Kizil, Höhle 219 (Ajātaśatru-Höhle), Klagende Königsfamilie, Inv.-Nr. III 8881, Detail, Vorzustand © S. Nitsche, 2017

Die Malerei wurde auf hellbraunem, mit Strohhäckseln armierten Lehmputz und einer aufliegenden, dünnen Grundierung ausgeführt. Vorherrschende Farben sind Braun, Grün und Blau. Vor einem braunen Hintergrund mit blauen und weißen Dekorationen sitzen die beiden blau gewandeten Arhats und werden von grünen Flammen umgeben. Auch in der Balkonszene dominieren diese drei Farbtöne. Es ist zu vermuten, dass das Farbspektrum der Malerei ursprünglich etwas breiter war, jedoch vereinzelte Pigmente und Farbstoffe wie beispielsweise Gelb durch fehlende Alterungsbeständigkeit mit der Zeit verloren gingen oder verblassten.

Insgesamt wurde die Malerei im Zuge der Abnahme in neun Platten geteilt. Bei der Führung der Sägeschnitte achteten die Bearbeiter darauf, die Malereien szenenweise zu unterteilen. Bedingt durch die Größe und Fülle der Figuren im oberen Abschnitt, verlaufen die Sägeschnitte hier jedoch auch durch figürliche Darstellungen. Alle abgenommenen Wandmalereisegmente wurden während der ersten Restaurierung vermutlich in den 20er oder 30er Jahren in metallarmierte Gipsträger eingebettet. Eine historische Aufnahme zeigt den Zustand nach der ersten Restaurierung (**Abb. 4**).

Auffällig ist, dass der originale, vermutlich monochrom bemalte, untere Bildstreifen nicht von der Höhlenwand abgenommen und auch bei der Restaurierung für die Präsentation im Völkerkundemuseum nicht rekonstruiert wurde. Dies verändert die Wahrnehmung der Wandsituation, wie sie *in situ* ursprünglich vorgefunden wurde, deutlich. Die ursprüngliche Nische der Wand erschien so in der damaligen Präsentation als Türöffnung.

Vermutlich kam es durch die Beschädigung des Museums für Völkerkunde während des 2. Weltkrieges zu erneuten großflächigen Verlusten des Bestandes. So fehlten nach dem Krieg vier der ehemals neun Bildplatten und das Gesims. Auch innerhalb der erhaltenen Platten kam es zu zusätzlichen Fehlstellen. Dokumentationen im Museum für Asiatische Kunst belegen Restaurierungen der 70er Jahre. So wurden die beiden erhaltenen Platten der Balkonszene aus den vorliegenden Bruchstücken neu zusammengesetzt. Dabei ist auch die Nische zu schmal rekonstruiert worden, so dass sich das ehemals mittlere

5 Vgl. Grünwedel 1912: 143.
6 Grünwedel 1912: 145.
7 Vgl. Zin 2020: 237.

Abb. 4 Kizil, Höhle 219 (Ajātaśatru-Höhle), Inv.-Nr. III 8881, Wandmalerei-Gesamtaufnahme aus der Vorkriegszeit, Foto-Nr. B 199 © Staatliche Museen zu Berlin, Museum für Asiatische Kunst

Bild der Balkonszene nun am rechten Bildrand befindet (**Abb. 5**). Dadurch wies die gesamte Darstellung der Malerei unkorrekte Proportionen auf.

Die Voruntersuchung und Kartierung der Wandmalerei ergaben, dass die drei Bildplatten der unteren beiden Reihen gut erhalten waren. Abgesehen von einigen Putzergänzungen im Inneren war der originale Putz dort großflächig überkommen. Die beiden erhaltenen Malereiplatten der Balkonszene wiesen deutlich weniger originale Substanz auf. Alle verlorenen Putzflächen waren putzsichtig ergänzt. In einigen Bereichen überlagerten die Kittungen die originalen Putzflanken. Viele Putzergänzungen waren mit einer Volltonretusche geschlossen. Meist beschränkte sich die Retusche auf die hinzugefügten Bereiche. In einigen Zonen verlief sie jedoch auch auf dem originalen Bestand.

Die fünf erhaltenen Bildplatten wiesen alle ähnliche Schadensphänomene auf. Das Ausmaß der einzelnen Schäden variierte jedoch stark. So wurden Putzfehlstellen, Risse, Putzhohlstellen, Malschichtfehlstellen, großflächige Malschichtabhebungen und gedünnte Malschichten verzeichnet (**Abb. 6**). Oberflächenglanz tritt auf allen Platten mit erhaltener Malerei partiell auf. Vereinzelte Phänomene waren Verfärbungen und Druckstellen im Lehmputz. Um den erhaltenen Bestand der wertvollen Malereien zu schützen und eine neue Präsentation im Humboldt Forum zu ermöglichen, war zunächst eine Konservierung und Entrestaurierung, d.h. Entfernung potentiell schädigender, durch frühere Restaurierungen eingefügter Materialien, notwendig. Grundlage für die Maßnahmen und die Entwicklung eines Konzeptes bildeten die Kartierungen der Altrestaurierungen und der Schäden. Durch das Wissen über Bestand, Zustand und Schadensursachen konnten Handlungsbedarf, notwendige Arbeitsschritte und Umfang der Maßnahmen festgelegt werden. Voraussetzung zur Verhinderung weiterer Verluste ist die Sicherung des Bestandes und die Reduzierung von Schadfaktoren. Hierzu zählen die Sicherung des Bildträgers, Putz- und Malschichtsicherung, Reduzierung schädigender Altkittungen und die damit verbundene Abnahme ungeeigneter und häufig auf das Original verlaufender Altretuschen sowie die Reduzierung von zu dichten Oberflächenauflagen.

Bei der Entwicklung des Konzeptes konnte auf die Erfahrungen und Rezepte des Museums für Asiatische Kunst der letzten Jahre zurückgegriffen werden. Für jeden Arbeitsschritt wurden Testreihen und Probeflächen angelegt und die bekannten Rezepte an den Bedarf der

Abb. 5 Kizil, Höhle 219 (Ajātaśatru-Höhle), Inv.-Nr. III 8881, Wandmalerei-Gesamtaufnahme, Zustand vor der Konservierung, Entrestaurierung und Restaurierung © S. Nitsche, 2017

Abb. 6 Kizil, Höhle 219 (Ajātaśatru-Höhle), Arhat mit Flammen, Inv.-Nr. III 8881, Detail, Vorzustand, Schadensphänomene © S. Nitsche, 2017

einzelnen Malereien angepasst. Erst im Anschluss an all diese Vorarbeit konnte die Entrestaurierung und Konservierung beginnen. Mit größter Behutsamkeit, unter Verwendung von Lupenbrillen und Feinwerkzeugen wurden alle konservatorisch notwendigen Arbeitsschritte ausgeführt. Im Anschluss erfolgte die Restaurierung, d.h. Arbeitsschritte zur Ergänzung des Originalbestandes und zur Verbesserung der Erlebbarkeit des Kunstwerkes.

Hierzu entschieden die Beteiligten die einzelnen Malereiplatten auf zusätzlichen Hilfsträgern aus Aluminium wieder zusammenzufügen. Somit konnten weitestgehend die durch die Abnahme vom historischen Standort entstandenen Sägefugen reduziert und zum Teil bereits gebrochene Hilfsträger stabilisiert werden. Um die Möglichkeit der Transportierbarkeit des Wandmalereikomplexes weiterhin zu gewährleisten, wurden nicht alle Fugen verschlossen, da dies zu einem zu hohen Gewicht der Gesamtkonstruktion geführt hätte. Ziel der Restaurierung war es, die originale Wandsituation bestmöglich wieder herzustellen und erlebbar zu machen. Hierzu zählten die Verbreiterung der Nische, die Anfügung eines Gesimses und die Vermittlung der Nischensituation durch eine Sockelplatte.

In der Konservierung und Restaurierung gilt der allgemeine Grundsatz: „So viel wie nötig und so wenig wie möglich". Das heißt, dass die Eingriffe, besonders in die originale Substanz, vor dem Hintergrund der Notwendigkeit genau abgewogen werden müssen. Da die bearbeiteten Malereien in einem musealen Kontext präsentiert werden und der Betrachter hier die Möglichkeit hat, die Kunstwerke aus nächster Nähe zu betrachten, ergab sich der Wunsch nach einer Präsentation, die dem Besucher erlaubt, die Malerei weitestgehend vollständig zu erleben. Grundsatz einer Retusche oder Rekonstruktion in der Wandmalereirestaurierung ist stets, dass die ergänzten Malereibereiche bei genauerem Betrachten als solche ablesbar und zu erkennen sind. So darf nur ergänzt werden, was bekannt ist und rekonstruierbare Kittungen werden mittels Punkt- oder Strichretusche geschlossen. Diese fügen sich in die Malerei ein und schließen sie optisch. Punkt- oder Strichretuschen werden nur auf den Oberflächen der Kittungen ausgeführt, um die Authentizität der originalen Malerei, sowohl im Hinblick auf ihre Darstellung, als auch auf ihre Materialität zu wahren. Zonen, in denen die originale Malschicht gedünnt ist, verbleiben in ihrem gealterten Zustand. In Fällen in denen kleine, nicht kittbare Abplatzungen hell heraustreten, ist der Einsatz von sogenanntem *aqua sporca*, einer Schmutzwasserlasur, zu diskutieren, um eine optische Beruhigung des Zustandes zu ermöglichen. Um die Art, die Ausführung und das Ausmaß der geplanten Retuschen festzulegen, wurden auch hier Probeflächen angelegt und mit allen Beteiligten abgestimmt.

Auf Grund existierender Objektfotografien aus der Vorkriegszeit ergab sich der seltene Fall, dass Bildmaterial zu einigen Fehlstellen und Verlusten vorhanden war. Aus diesem Grund wurde sich für eine weiterreichende Retusche als üblich entschieden, die eine Rekonstruktion dieser fehlenden Bildbereiche vorsah.

Folgendes Konzept wurde erarbeitet:
- Einsatz von *aqua sporca*-Lasuren im Bereich kleinerer Ausplatzungen;
- feine Strichretusche rekonstruierbarer Abschnitte auf den Kittungen innerhalb der Malereiplatten (**Abb. 7, 8**);
- nicht rekonstruierbare Fehlstellen, sogenannte Primärschäden (bereits *in situ* vorhandene Malereifehlstellen) verbleiben putzsichtig (**Abb. 9**);

- Ergänzung verlorener Malereiplatten, die vor dem 2. Weltkrieg noch erhalten waren und fotografisch dokumentiert sind, mithilfe eines Fotodrucks.

Auf Grundlage von Empfehlungen durch den leitenden Restaurator Toralf Gabsch M.A. wurde ein Konzept erarbeitet, die fotografischen Aufnahmen in die Wandmalerei einzufügen und somit die verlorenen Wandmalereiplatten wieder zu integrieren. Wichtig waren hierbei ein möglichst harmonisches Gesamterscheinungsbild und eine Wiederherstellung der Ablesbarkeit der Darstellung. Dies konnte mit einer Methode, die Lehmputz und Fotodruck miteinander verbindet, erreicht werden. Die neu hergestellten Trägerplatten wurden zunächst mit einem in Farbigkeit

Abb. 7 Kizil, Höhle 13, Nonne, Inv.-Nr. III 8859b, Detail, Strichretusche © J. Schaer, 2020

und Beschaffenheit dem originalen Lehmputz angepassten lehmhaltigen Grundputz versehen. Die Fotografien der verlorenen Bildplatten erhielten eine digitale Bearbeitung und wurden im Anschluss auf dünnem, durchscheinendem Japanpapier gedruckt. Durch die Klebung der durchscheinenden Drucke auf den Putzuntergrund konnte der gewünschte Eindruck erzielt werden: Der Putzträger bleibt ästhetisch erlebbar, die Darstellungen schließen sich harmonisch und sämtliche Zutaten setzen sich dennoch deutlich von der originalen Wandmalerei ab. Durch die Rekonstruktion der ursprünglichen Wandsituation und dem Schließen der kriegsbedingten Fehlstellen, kann die herausragende Wandmalerei nun an ihrem neuen Ausstellungsort wieder gewürdigt werden (**Abb. 10, 11**).

Abb. 8 Kizil, Höhle 219 (Ajātaśatru-Höhle), Arhat mit Flammen, Inv.-Nr. III 8881, Detail, Strichretusche © M. Fortmann, 2020

Abb. 9 Kizil, Höhle 219 (Ajātaśatru-Höhle), Arhat mit Flammen, Inv.-Nr. III 8881 Detail, Zustand nach der Restaurierung © M. Fortmann, 2020

Bibliographie

Grünwedel, Albert (1912) *Altbuddhistische Kultstätten in Chinesisch-Turkistan: Bericht über archäologische Arbeiten von 1906 bis 1907 bei Kuča, Qarašahr und in der Oase Turfan.* Berlin (Königlich Preussische Turfan-Expeditionen).

Abb. 10 Kizil, Höhle 219 (Ajātaśatru-Höhle), Arhat mit Flammen, Inv-Nr. III 8881, Detail, Zwischenzustand nach Retusche und Beklebung Fotodruck © M. Fortmann, 2020

Abb. 11 Kizil, Höhle 219 (Ajātaśatru-Höhle), Wandmalerei-Gesamtaufnahme, Zustand nach der Konservierung und Restaurierung © M. Fortmann, 2021

van Tangerloo, Aloïs, Michael Knüppel & Toralf Gabsch (2012) Theodor Bartus – Forschungsreisender, Museumstechniker und Restaurator, In: Toralf Gabsch & Staatliche Museen zu Berlin (Hgg.), *Auf Grünwedels Spuren: Restaurierung und Forschung an zentralasiatischen Wandmalereien*. Leipzig: 30–49.

Zin, Monika (2020) *Representations of the Parinirvāṇa Story Cycle in Kucha*. New Delhi (Leipzig Kucha Studies, 2).

English Summary

The new permanent exhibition of the Museum für Asiatische Kunst Berlin (Asian Art Museum) in the Humboldt Forum presents five Buddhist wall paintings from the 6th and 7th centuries CE. The past centuries have left traces on the artworks. After examining the paintings, a concept for conservation and restoration was developed and implemented. The primary requirement of such a measure is the protection and preservation of the original substance. As a result, the main priority lies on the conservation of the artwork. Only then is a decision made about the colour integration of missing parts. In accordance with today's restoration ethics, the following applies here: The focus is always on keeping the genuine work of art. Retouching or inserting missing parts can only support the recognisability, but must never become a work of art in its own right. Thus, the integration of imperfections represents a balancing act between the appreciation of the original work of art and the preservation and development of its aesthetic value.

„Für die Seele meines Vaters ... Kara Totok" – Die Darstellung eines hohen, uigurischen Würdenträgers auf einer Tempelfahne aus Kocho

Thomas Arens

Einleitung

Unter den archäologischen Objekten der Turfan-Sammlung des Museums für Asiatische Kunst, befinden sich ca. 924 Textilobjekte. Zu ihnen gehören Fragmente bemalter, oder in verschiedenen Techniken bestickter Seiden- und Baumwollgewebe ebenso wie Fragmente von 794 Tempelfahnen aus der Zeit vom 6. bis in das 14. Jahrhundert.[1] Eine Tempelfahne mit der Darstellung eines uigurischen Würdenträgers stellt das wohl eindrucksvollste Beispiel innerhalb dieser Sammlungsgruppe dar (**Abb. 1, 2**). Aus diesem Grunde wurde es, gemeinsam mit vierundzwanzig anderen Textilobjekten, für die Eröffnungspräsentation im Humboldt Forum ausgewählt.[2]

Zur Geschichte

Die bedeutende Sammlung archäologischer Objekte, Wandmalereien, Handschriften und Textilien, von Fundstätten entlang der nördlichen Seidenstraße, gründet sich auf vier deutsche Expeditionen in den Jahren 1902 bis 1914. Ziel waren Ruinen-Stätten und buddhistische Höhlentempelanlagen in Zentralasien (heute Uigurisches Autonomes Gebiet Xinjiang, Volksrepublik China). Die Forschungsreisen wurden von Albert Grünwedel, dem damaligen Direktor der Indischen Abteilung des Museums für Völkerkunde, Berlin und von Albert von Le Coq geleitet. Die Funde wurden ebendort aufbewahrt und ausgestellt, sind aber nach der Gründung des Museums für Indische Kunst im Jahre 1963 in dessen Sammlungen überführt worden und werden bis heute am Standort des Museums für Asiatische Kunst in Berlin-Dahlem aufbewahrt.[3] Die hier beschriebene Tempelfahne mit der Inventarnummer III 4524 wurde bereits im Rahmen der ersten Expedition in der Oase Turfan entdeckt und nach Berlin gebracht.

Die Ruinenstadt Kocho (auch Chotscho, Qočo, Gaochang, Karachodscha, Idukutschahri, Dakianus) befindet sich 30 km südöstlich der Stadt Turfan. Sie wurde vermutlich im 1. vorchristlichen Jahrhundert erbaut und ab dem 14 Jh. verlassen und langsam zerstört.[4] Kocho selbst war eine weiträumige alte Tempel- und Palaststadt umgeben von einer dicken ca. 15 m hohen Mauer aus gestampftem Lehm, die mit ursprünglich fünf Torbauten versehen war. Im Inneren befanden sich hunderte religiöser Gebäude, Tempel, Klöster, Grabmale und Paläste. Ab dem 8.–9. Jh. n. Chr. übernahmen Uiguren die Herrschaft über die Region Turfan. Kocho wurde die Hauptstadt ihres Königreichs. Manichäismus war einmalig auf der Welt Staatsreligion bei den Uiguren bis zum späten 10. bis frühen 11. Jahrhundert, danach wechselten auch die Herrscher zum Buddhismus.

Interessant ist, dass die Tempelfahne in der Ruine Alpha geborgen wurde: eine Stätte, die neben Funden buddhistischer Kunst besonders durch manichäische Fragmente beeindruckte.[5]

1 Für die Zahl der Tempelfahnen und Tempelfahne Fragmente siehe Bhattacharya-Haesner 2003: 9.

2 Über die neue Dauerausstellung im Kuppelraum des Berliner Schloss siehe Russell-Smith 2022.

3 Zur Sammlungsgeschichte des Museums für Indische Kunst siehe Yaldiz 2009. Die Sammlung wurde 2006 mit dem Museum für Ostasiatische Kunst vereinigt zum Museum für Asiatische Kunst. Seit Herbst 2021 zeigt das Museum seine neue Dauerpräsentation und wechselnde Inszenierungen im Berliner Humboldt Forum.

4 Ein von der Gerda Henkel Stiftung gefördertes Projekt hat durch systematischen Vergleich von Fotos der Turfan-Expeditionen mit Fotos von 2015 die großen Änderungen in den Ruinen demonstriert und insbesondere die Funde aus Holz untersucht. Siehe Russell-Smith/Konczak 2016.

5 Zu Kocho und den Funden der Ruine Alpha siehe auch Grünwedel 1906: 55–73, Dreyer 2015.

Zum Objekt

Das in sehr hoher, künstlerischer Qualität beidseitig bemalte Objekt wird in das 10. bis 12. Jahrhundert datiert.[6] Die ursprüngliche Länge des Objektes ist aufgrund des fragmentarischen Erhaltungszustandes nicht mehr feststellbar und beträgt heute 145 cm, die maximale Breite liegt bei 51,5 cm. Beidseitig weist die Fahne uigurische Inschriften auf (**Abb. 3**). Sie besagen, dass es sich bei dem Dargestellten um eine hochgestellte Persönlichkeit namens „Kara Totok" handelt. Die Kleidung und der Titel „Totok" bezeichnen die Funktion als hohen Minister.[7] Es handelt sich bei dem Dargestellten also vermutlich um eine hochrangige, politische Persönlichkeit des uigurischen Königreiches. Die Fahne wurde zum Gedenken des Verstorbenen von seinen beiden Söhnen gestiftet. Diese sind als Kinder links und rechts neben der Hauptfigur ebenfalls abgebildet.[8]

Der mit langen, grauen Haaren und grauem Bart Portraitierte, trägt ein reich gemustertes, bodenlanges Gewand. An einem Gürtel sind diverse Werkzeuge und Gebrauchsutensilien befestigt.[9] Die auffällige, kronenartige Kopfbedeckung schließt mit einem Kinnband (**Abb. 4**). Rückwärtig fällt ein Tuch bis auf die Schultern herab. Schwarze hohe Stiefel vervollständigen die Kleidung. Die langstielige Päonie in seinen Händen weist ihn als bereits Verstorbenen aus.

Abb. 1 Gedenkfahne für Kara Totok, Kocho, Xinjiang, China, 10.–12. Jh., Baumwolle, bemalt. Museum für Asiatische Kunst Inv.-Nr. III 4524. Zustand vor der Restaurierung © Staatliche Museen zu Berlin, Museum für Asiatische Kunst / Thomas Arens

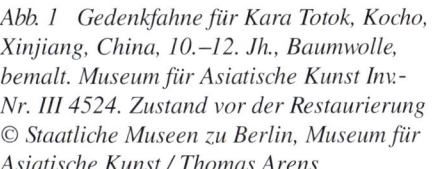

Abb. 2 Objekt auf Trägerplatte, Endzustand © Staatliche Museen zu Berlin, Museum für Asiatische Kunst / Thomas Arens

6 Die Datierung der buddhistischen Kunst der Uiguren ist bis heute umstritten.

7 Dazu schreibt Bhattacharya-Haesner: „This Type B: 2:2 banner, illustrating the portrait of a Uigur dignitary, well known as 'the Uigur Prince', is one of the rarest painted banners in the Collection. Except for a little change on its reverse, both sides of this banner depict the same theme, including the ornamental motifs. The triangular head with side-borders has a loop at its apex for suspension. The body of the banner is damaged and parts are missing. Of the four plain-buff legs or bottom-streamers, only three are partly extant. The arms or side-streamers are missing." Kat No. 497, S. 352. Inschrift: S. 464–465 (Übersetzung von Peter Zieme).

8 Bhatacharya-Haesner 2003: 355.

9 Nach Yaldiz ein Behälter für Eßstäbchen, Stifte und Feuersteine, ein Tabakbeutel und Amulette. Yaldiz et.al. 2000: 247.

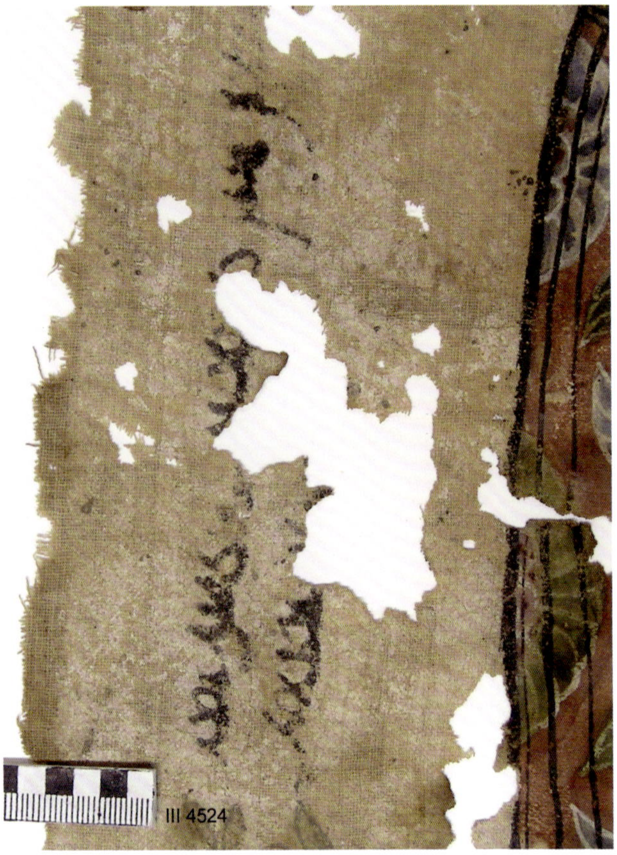

Abb. 3 Detail der uigurischen Inschrift, Vorzustand © Staatliche Museen zu Berlin, Museum für Asiatische Kunst / Thomas Arens

Abb. 4 Detail des Kopfes, Vorzustand, Rückansicht © Staatliche Museen zu Berlin, Museum für Asiatische Kunst / Thomas Arens

Innerhalb des Fahnenkopfes erscheint, ungewöhnlich klein, in einer von Blüten umgebenen Mandorla, ein Buddha.[10] In blaue und rote Gewänder gehüllt, sitzt er in meditativer Haltung auf einem Lotospodest. Dieser Bereich ist, durch eine zackenartige Borte vom Mittelfeld getrennt, wie ein Baldachin gestaltet. Das Motiv auf beiden Seiten der Fahne ist, bis auf wenige Abwandlungen, gleich.

Technologischer Aufbau

Die Tempelfahne setzt sich aus fünf Elementen zusammen.[11] Das mittlere Bildfeld, das nach oben in einer Spitze abschließt, die blendenartige Einfassung des „Fahnenkopfes“ mit erhaltener Schlaufe zur Aufhängung. Darüber hinaus seitlich am „Fahnenkopf“ fixierte, frei herabhängende Bänder (hier fehlend) und die vier Bänder des unteren Abschlusses, die möglicherweise durch eine Holzleiste miteinander verbunden und beschwert waren.

Technologische Untersuchungen haben ergeben, dass für die Fertigung der Fahne leinwandbindiges Baumwollgewebe in unterschiedlicher Qualität verwendet wurde. Alle Nähte sind mit einfachen Stichen von Hand ausgeführt.

Für die Malerei wurden zumeist Pigmentfarben verwendet. Unter dem Mikroskop erscheint die Malschicht sehr pastos auf dem Gewebe aufliegend. Nur wenige Details, wie schwarze Konturstriche wirken wie lasiert, auf diese Schichten aufgetragen. Blau, Grün- und Rottöne dominieren, sehr feine schwarze Linien akzentuieren Haar- und Barttracht. Der Hintergrund des Mittelfeldes war ursprünglich in Weiß gehalten. Die Verwendung ei-

10 „This banner… is both a memorial and a portrayal banner. This type is found in Turfan only. It illustrates the portrait of a Uigur noble person on the body of the banner instead of a deity, although its head shows Amitābha seated in meditation.“ Bhattacharya-Haesner 2003: 355. Siehe auch Russell-Smith 2005: 26–27, Gulácsi 2015 und Russell-Smith 2021 über die Ähnlichkeiten zu manichäischen Tempelfahnen in der Berliner Sammlung.

11 Zum Aufbau von Tempelfahnen Bhattacharya-Haesner 2003: 38–40.

ner Grundierung ist aufgrund des eher groben Malgrundes, zu vermuten.

Wünschenswert wären weiterführende, naturwissenschaftliche Analysen zur näheren Bestimmung der verwendeten Mal- und Grundiermittel.

Erhaltungszustand

Natürliche Alterung, klimatische Bedingungen und Umwelteinflüsse am Fundort über mehrere Jahrhunderte haben unübersehbare Spuren am Objekt hinterlassen. Die textilen Bestandteile sind partiell fleckig verbräunt, brüchig und es ist zu erheblichen Materialverlusten gekommen. Zahlreiche Schad- und Fehlstellen führten zu einer Destabilisierung des gesamten Fahnenkörpers und erschwerten die Lesbarkeit der Darstellungen.

Die Malschichten, sofern erhalten, weisen grundsätzlich Risse, Abrieb und Abplatzungen auf. Die weiße Malschicht des Hintergrundes ist großflächig verloren. Besonders auffällig ist der musterartige Ausfall von Gewebeflächen mit ehemals grüner Bemalung. Hier ist zu vermuten, dass das Farbmittel Bestandteile von Kupfer enthält. In Verbindung mit Feuchtigkeit kommt es zu chemischen Reaktionen zwischen den Kupferpigmenten (Kupferionen) und der Zellulose als Hauptbestandteil der Baumwolle. Es entstehen Säuren, die den molekularen Aufbau der Zellulose soweit abbauen können, bis diese zerfällt.

Das Objekt wurde über einen sehr langen Zeitraum in der Dauerausstellung des ehemaligen Museums für Indische Kunst senkrecht hängend gezeigt. Um beide Seiten der Fahne sichtbar zu belassen, war diese zwischen zwei Acrylglasscheiben mit formgenauer Vertiefung gelegt worden. Um das Objekt in Position zu halten, ist bei dieser Art der Montage dennoch ein gewisser Druck notwendig. Dieser Druck führt auf Dauer unweigerlich zu Schäden am hochfragilen Material. Aus diesem Grunde wurde beschlossen diese Art der Präsentation im Museum für Asiatische Kunst nicht wieder zu verwenden. Die Malerei wurde schon 2008 aus der Dauerausstellung aus diesem Grund auf Wunsch der Kuratorin entfernt und im Depot in Dahlem aufbewahrt.[12]

12 Mit der Vereinigung der beiden Museen, dem Museum für Indische Kunst und dem Museum für Ostasiatische Kunst, gibt es mehr Austausch über Malerei auf Seide und anderen Textilien und die Vorgabe diese auch aus konservatorischen Gründen regelmäßig zu wechseln.

Restaurierungskonzept

Das Konzept zur Restaurierung eines Objektes wird einer jeden konservatorischen/ restauratorischen Bearbeitung vorangestellt. Sie formuliert das Vorgehen und das Ziel und schafft somit eine Übersicht und Erläuterungen über die anzuwendenden Methoden.

In ihrem fragilen und stark geschädigten Vorzustand war die Tempelfahne in keinem ausstellungsfähigen Zustand (**Abb. 1**). Das Objekt musste vorrangig stabilisiert und gesichert werden. Darüber hinaus, inspiriert von den Ergänzungen an den neu restaurierten Wandmalereien wünschte sich die zuständige Kuratorin, Frau Dr. L Russell-Smith auch in diesem Fall die Entwicklung einer Methode, welche die Erscheinung der Malerei mehr an den Originalzustand annähert. Die Lösung waren farblich angepasste Unterlegungen und Ergänzungen aus Baumwollgeweben (**Abb. 5**): diese können zu einer Verbesserung der Lesbarkeit und somit zu einer wiederhergestellten ästhetischen Gesamterscheinung führen. In welchem Ausmaß Ergänzungen eingesetzt werden, muss bei jeder Restaurierung sorgfältig abgewogen werden. Die bei dem vorliegenden Objekt vorgenommenen Ergänzungen erfolgten in enger Absprache mit der Kuratorin. Grundsätzlich gilt die Regel der so genannten Reversibilität. Jede Restaurierungsmaßnahme muss jederzeit zurückgenommen werden können.

Auch Überlegungen zu Art und Weise der Präsentation sind Bestandteil des Konzeptes. Sie umfassen z. B. Trägerplatten oder Stützkonstruktionen. Konservatorische Vorgaben im Hinblick auf Klima, Temperatur und Licht werden formuliert. Sie folgen engen Grenzen zum Schutz des Objektes.

Restaurierung

Von der Möglichkeit, die Tempelfahne weiterhin von beiden Seiten sichtbar in der Ausstellung zu präsentieren, musste Abstand genommen werden. Aus gestalterischen Gründen wird das Objekt stattdessen auf einer schrägen Fläche von 5° Grad in einer Vitrine gezeigt. Obwohl nun eine Schauseite festgelegt wurde, muss die Abseite für mögliche Forschungen weiterhin zugänglich bleiben. Alle nachfolgend durchgeführten Restaurierungsarbeiten richten sich entsprechend nach dieser Vorgabe.

Zunächst wurde das Objekt aus seiner bisherigen Montage aus Acrylglas entnommen. In dem Bereich der Vertiefung fanden sich, wie erwartet, Bruchstücke von Fasermaterial und winzige Farbpartikel aus den

Malschichten. Aus diesem Grunde, und weil Fahnenkopf und Fahnenkörper nur noch an einer einzigen Stelle miteinander verbunden sind, musste jede Bewegung mit äußerster Vorsicht durchgeführt werden. Bei der anschließenden Reinigung unter der hohen Vergrößerung eines Auflichtmikroskops, wurden weitere aufliegende Fasern und Stäube mittels stark reduzierter Absaugung schonend entfernt.

Für die weiteren Schritte wurden verschiedene Seiden- und Baumwollgewebe, sowie feinster Nähfaden aus Seide benötigt. Die Textilrestaurierung kann dabei auf Methoden zurückgreifen, die es erlauben, jeden gewünschten Farbton exakt zum Objekt passend einzufärben. Es können sowohl ganze Gewebestücke eingefärbt, als auch einzelne Bereiche in einer speziellen Technik partiell bemalt werden. Das Material wird immer so gewählt, dass es sich dem Original weitestgehend anpasst. Bei Geweben bedeutet dies, gleiche Webbindung, gleiche Anzahl der Fäden pro Zentimeter und gleiche Fadendrehung.

Die Stabilisierung und Verbindung von Fahnenkopf und Fahnenkörper erfolgte unterseitig mit einem sehr transparenten Seidengewebe. Optisch ist dieses Gewebe aufgrund seiner lockeren Webart kaum wahrnehmbar. Es wurde nähtechnisch durch Vorstiche fixiert. Dabei musste darauf geachtet werden, in keinem Fall die brüchigen Malschichten zu durchstechen. Dies hätte zwangsläufig zu erneuten Materialverlusten geführt. Genutzt wurden Bereiche, in denen die Malschicht überwiegend abgerieben ist, und das Grundgewebe frei liegt.

Fehlstellen in textilen Objekten werden üblicherweise optisch geschlossen, indem ein passend eingefärbtes Gewebe hinterlegt, und nähtechnisch mit dem Objekt verbunden wird. Dieses ist jedoch nicht sinnvoll, wenn zwei Schauseiten, wie bei dem vorliegenden Objekt, zugänglich bleiben müssen. Aus diesem Grunde wurde aus einem Kunststoffmaterial eine der Form des Objektes entsprechende Trägerplatte angefertigt und mit einem Baumwollgewebe bezogen. Auf diesem Gewebe wurden nun mit Hilfe einer Schablone, entsprechend der Fehlstellen in der Fahne, alle Bereiche entweder partiell eingefärbt, oder eingefärbte Gewebestücke nähtechnisch fixiert. Neben den zahlreichen Fehlstellen, die durch eine einfarbige Fläche optisch geschlossen werden konnten, gibt es einen besonderen Verlust. Stiel und Blätter der Päonie, die der Dargestellte in der Hand hält, sind partiell verloren. Nach langer Überlegung und dem unbefriedigenden Versuch, diese Stelle mit einer einfarbigen Unterlegung zu schließen, wurde beschlossen, die fehlenden Teile des Stieles und der Blätter malerisch zu ergänzen.

Abb. 5 Objektträgerplatte mit farbigen Ergänzungen aus Baumwollgewebe, Zwischenzustand © Staatliche Museen zu Berlin, Museum für Asiatische Kunst / Thomas Arens

Das durch Unterlegung nunmehr gesicherte Objekt liegt ohne feste Fixierung auf der formgenauen Unterlage mit den positionierten, eingefärbten Fehlstellen. Somit bleibt die Rückseite, wie gewünscht, jederzeit zugänglich. Lediglich einige von Fehlstelle zu Fehlstelle gespannte, und im Bezugsstoff des Trägers fixierte Seidenfäden sichern die Fahne. Aus dem Rahmen aus lackiertem Kunststoff ist die Form der Fahne als Vertiefung ausgefräst. In dieser Vertiefung liegt die Trägerplatte des Objektes. Diese verdeckt auch kreisrunde Aussparungen, die in den Boden eingearbeitet sind. Hier hinein kommen starke Neodym-Magnete, die das montierte Objekt auf der schrägen Vitrinenrückwand aus Stahl unsichtbar in Position halten. Die Trägerplatten dienen nicht nur der Präsentation, mit ihnen wird das Objekt transportiert und auch deponiert, so dass es nicht mehr notwendig ist, das empfindliche Textil selbst zu berühren oder zu bewegen.

Zusammen mit 21 anderen Textilobjekten aus der Turfan-Sammlung des Museums für Asiatische Kunst, ist der „Uigurische Fürst“ aktuell in der Ausstellung des

Humboldt Forums zu sehen. Da Textilien sehr empfindlich auf Lichteinwirkung reagieren, ist die Helligkeit im Raum sehr gedämpft. Trotzdem wird auf eine Begrenzung der Ausstellungsdauer und regelmäßigen Wechsel geachtet, so dass die Objekte letztendlich in die Studiensammlung in Dahlem zurückkehren, wo sie bei völliger Dunkelheit sicher verwahrt werden können.

Danksagung

Ich danke Lilla Russell-Smith und Uta Schröder für ihre Ergänzungen.

Bibliographie

Bhattacharya-Haesner, Chhaya (2003) *Central Asian Temple Banners in the Turfan Collection of the Museum für Indische Kunst, Berlin*. Berlin.

Dreyer, Caren (2015) *Abenteuer Seidenstraße: Die Berliner Turfan-Expeditionen 1902–1914*. Berlin.

Grünwedel, Albert (1906) *Bericht über Archäologische Arbeiten in Idikutschari und Umgebung im Winter 1902–1903*. München.

Gulácsi, Zs. (2018) The Manichaean Roots of a Pure Land Banner from Uygur Kocho (III 4524) in the Asian Art Museum, Berlin, *Language, Society, and Religion in the World of the Turks: Festschrift for Larry Clark at Seventy-Five,* Zs. Gulácsi (ed.), Turnhout: 337–376 *(Silk Road Studies 19).*

Le Coq, A.v. (1924) *Die buddhistische Spätantike in Mittelasien, Band III: Die Wandmalereien*. Berlin: 45–46, pl. 17.

Russell-Smith, Lilla (2005): *Uygur Patronage in Dunhuang: Regional Art Centres on the Northern Silk Road in the Tenth and Eleventh Centuries.* Leiden.

Russell-Smith, Lilla (2021): Gedenkfahne für Kara Totok, *Humboldt Forum: Ethnologisches Museum, Museum für Asiatische Kunst (Prestel Führer),* Berlin: 116–117.

Russell-Smith, Lilla (2022): A Journey on the Northern Silk Road, Under the Dome in the Humboldt Forum, *Orientations* vol. 53 no. 2 (Hong Kong): 56–65.

Russell-Smith, Lilla & Konczak, Ines (2016) *The Ruins of Kocho: Traces of Wooden Architecture on the Ancient Silk Road*. Berlin.

Yaldiz, Marianne (2009) Verantwortung und Leidenschaft – das Museum für Indische Kunst und seine Sammler. *Zum Lob der Sammler. Die Staatlichen Museen zu Berlin und ihre Sammler,* Andrea Bärnreuther & Peter-Klaus Schuster (Hgs.). Berlin: 334–347.

Yaldiz, Marianne et.al. (2000) Magische Götterwelten – Werke aus dem Museum für Indische Kunst. Berlin: Staatliche Museen zu Berlin – Preußischer Kulturbesitz.

English Summary

A painted memorial banner with the depiction of an Uyghur high ranking official is one of the most impressive banner paintings, from to the so-called „Turfan-Collection“ of the Museum für Asiatische Kunst Berlin (Asian Art Museum). The object was found in the Turfan region (today Uyghur Autonomous Region Xinjiang, People's Republic of China) and brought to Berlin in 1902.

An inscription identifies the represented person as Kara Totok, a high ranking Minister. In commemoration of their father, his two sons, also pictured, donated the banner, hoping to help him to achieve a better rebirth in the Pure Land.

The depiction of a secular dignitary as the main motive, with only small depiction of a Buddha figure in the banner's headpiece, reflects the transition from the Manichaean to the Buddhist religion in the late 10th, early 11th century in the Uyghur kingdom.

The article describes the conservation method that allows to close the damaged areas, thereby giving a better visitor experience. This painting is part of the first presentation in the exhibition of the Museum für Asiatische Kunst in the Humboldt Forum.

A 'Pensive Bodhisatva' from Takht-i-Bahi, Formerly in the Museum für Völkerkunde, Berlin: Object History and Art Historical Study

Corinna Wessels-Mevissen

Introduction

A remarkably rare Bodhisatva image from Gandhāra was offered for sale to the Königliches Museum für Völkerkunde (Royal Museum of Ethnology), Berlin, in August 1910, together with a handsome standing Buddha stele, both carved in the usual schist.[1] As the findspot of both objects, the well-known Buddhist hill monastery of Takht-i-Bahi, now in Pakistan, was named. The offer was made during a period when the museum's collections were being continuously augmented,[2] well before World War I. The stele under discussion presents a heavily adorned seated Bodhisatva, with the lower portions of his legs and the throne missing (**Figs. 1, 2**)[3]. Its most significant feature is a peculiar kind of 'pointing gesture', whereby the index finger of his proper right hand is extended and touches the lower portion of his turban. With his head inclined in the same direction, his right side, a sentiment of melancholy is generally evoked in the viewer. Such a notion must have been behind the cognomen that was subsequently coined, i.e. 'Mourning (*Trauernder*) Avalokiteśvara'.[4] After World War I, the museum's heyday continued seamlessly, during a peacetime period of 21 years. However, when Nazi Germany commenced World War II in 1939 and the conflicts led to a huge backlash on the aggressor, the museum's movable holdings had to be evacuated from the building, which had fallen under the threat of destruction. After the Ger-

Fig. 1 'Pensive Bodhisatva', Takht-i-Bahi (Pakistan), 3rd century, schist (with an old plaster lining under the proper right knee), 67 x 45 x 16 cm, State Hermitage Museum, St Petersburg (Russian Federation), inv. no. ВДсэ-595

1 The Buddha image (old acc. no. IC 36835; new acc. no. I 77) will not be dealt with here. It remained in Berlin and is still a major attraction of the Museum für Asiatische Kunst, Staatliche Museen zu Berlin (Asian Art Museum, State Museums of Berlin). Its new galleries, since September 2021, are located in the reconstructed Berlin city palace (Berliner Stadtschloss), now conceived as the Humboldt Forum, a state of the art museum, among other activities, inviting international dialogues on questions of cultural heritage with a wide range of stakeholders.

2 For the section referred to as Indian department (*Indische Abteilung*, since 1904), see Schneider 2018: 220–221.

3 Selected earlier publications are Le Coq 1922: 19; pl. 3; Dreyer *et al.* 2002: 38–39, acc. no. IC 36836.

4 Le Coq 1922: 19 (Der sogenannte "trauernde Avalokiteśvara"); Berlin 1926: 6 (Der "trauernde Bodhisattva Avalokiteśvara"). Quotation marks were inserted to indicate the cognomen.

man capitulation on 8/9 May 1945, a large number of provisionally sheltered museum objects were collected from the Zoo flak tower where the stele had been kept, relocating these to the Soviet Union. Thus, the Bodhisatva's fate took a rather unexpected turn, and it was not publicly shown for several decades. Meanwhile, it is on view in the South Asian galleries of the State Hermitage Museum, St Petersburg. The present study does not include details of the object history after the war ended in 1945.

In the following, I shall discuss several aspects of this exceptional relief sculpture, which conforms to the overall type of the 'Pensive',[5] or 'Contemplative', Bodhisatva,

Fig. 2 'Pensive Bodhisatva' (as in Fig. 1), photograph, in or before August 1910, taken at Torquay (UK), on behalf of Elizabeth Elsmie, Zenodo repository (https://doi.org/10.5281/zenodo.438296) © Department of Asia, British Museum, London, Creative Commons 4.0

if one accepts such a general, necessarily simplified, term. This rather loosely defined iconographic concept was in vogue throughout large parts of Asia, from c. 3rd century up to the 7th century.[6] Certain morphological ramifications can be observed throughout. The overall type quickly spread to regions further to the northeast and the Far East, though the exact chronology at Gandhāra and the functioning of the network of sites en route are not yet well understood. Even beyond the 7th/8th centuries, reminiscences of the peculiar physical attitude, involving one of the hands held close to the head, and an asymmetrical sitting posture, were perpetuated by certain forms of Avalokiteśvara and related Bodhisatva imagery.[7] An answer to the important question whether the specimen under discussion should be referred to as Avalokiteśvara will be given on the basis of the latest academic discourse.

First (1871), second (1874), and third acquisition (1910)

On 13 August 1910, an elderly lady based in Torquay, a seaside town in southern England, wrote a detailed letter to the director of the "Berlin Museum",[8] in a self-assured handwriting and confident tone, explaining that she would like to part with two exquisite Gandhāran sculptures from Takht-i-Bahi, then in British India. The objects referred to were a seated Bodhisatva and a standing Buddha, with each of them described in a short appraisal by J. Lockwood Kipling (1837–1911), former principal curator of the Lahore Museum and father of the well-known writer Rudyard Kipling. A photograph of each object accompanied her first letter (cf. **Fig. 2**)[9]. The potential seller was Elizabeth Elsmie (1840–1928), widow of the Scotsman George R. Elsmie (1838–1909), who had been employed by the British Indian Civil Service for 35 years, as the title of his autobiography of 1908 proudly stated.[10] More letters were exchanged, as Mrs Elsmie had not yet mentioned her asking price. After the initial interest had been aroused, she asked £90 for the two sculptures, an extraordinarily high price at the time,

5 More precisely, 'pensive' should be understood as a short form of 'pensive attitude', the details of which may vary to some degree. Overall, it involves certain postures of almost every part of the body.

6 See Lee 1993, based on her PhD thesis of 1984.

7 For an instructive example from Gandhāra itself (probably, Swat), see Jongeward 2019: 152, cat. no. 126.

8 She must have adopted the manner in which she referred to the Royal Museum of Ethnology (and, more precisely, its Indian department, which had a separate director) using the simplified term "Berlin Museum" from scholarly circles in the UK, who would have assumed that their contacts knew the correct reference.

9 The original photographs are not preserved in the museum archive. (Information given by Caren Dreyer, in her email of 25 February 2022.)

10 Elsmie 1908.

Fig. 3 'Pensive Bodhisatva' (as in Figs. 1 and 2), permanent display from December 1926, Room II, Wall I, niche (above), Museum für Völkerkunde, Berlin, acc. no. IC 36836 © Staatliche Museen zu Berlin, Museum für Asiatische Kunst, photograph by Max Krajewsky, 1926

and equivalent to 1845 German Marks. Nevertheless, the other party immediately accepted, and on 29 August 1910, Albert von Le Coq responded positively, on behalf of the director of the Indische Abteilung (Indian department), Albert Grünwedel, expressing their enthusiasm for the new acquisitions: "The statues will find a place of honour amongst our collections of similar sculptures, and as, now that Mr Burgess [James Burgess, 1832–1916] unfortunately is precluded by his age to actively follow up his antiquarian studies, Prof. G[rünwedel] is the only person left, capable of drawing the last archaeological conclusions from a scientific study of these specimens. They will help the progress of sciences when added to this public collection".[11] In another message, of 13 September 1910, preserved in its neatly typed version, the former statement is strengthened even further: "The statues will be exhibited as the finest specimens in our modest Gandhara collection." However, the desire to assign appropriate places to the new gems of the exhibition could not be fulfilled before December 1926, when a well-designed display of the museum's Gandhāra and Central Asia ("Turfan") collections was inaugurated in the galleries on the ground floor that had been previously occupied by the spectacular archaeological finds by Heinrich Schliemann (**Fig. 3**).[12] Indeed, Albert von Le Coq had the opportunity to supervise the new installations in the two years of his directorship of the Indische Abteilung, 1923–1925, succeeding Albert Grünwedel.

Within the framework of provenance research, the question regarding the stele's origin and archaeological context is extremely important. In her first letter, Elizabeth Elsmie pointed out the well-known site of Takht-i-Bahi and revealed herself as knowledegable of the fact that the Museum für Völkerkunde in Berlin already housed other objects from this very site.[13] However, she just briefly stated that the stelae "were given" to her in 1874, when she had been at Peshawar, and that she "brought them home" to the UK in 1893.[14] As any further details of this first acquisition were lacking, the alleged place of origin retained a question mark.[15] While attempting to look beyond the apparently understated circumstances of her acquisition of 1874, I was able to link

11 Ethnologisches Museum, file no. I/MV 1048, E 1615/10, handwritten draft of a presumably typewritten letter.

12 The permanent display was rearranged from 1921, when Grünwedel retired, which was completed in December 1926, on the 40th anniversary of the Völkerkundemuseum. Only then was the Gandhāra collection exhibited adequately for the first time. According to the guidebook published on that occasion, the Buddha was displayed in Room III, to be entered first, and the Bodhisatva in Room II (Berlin 1926: 5–6). One of the few black-and-white plates illustrates the 'Elsmie Buddha', testifying to the extraordinary status it was assigned.

13 She had consulted "savants", naming in particular Aurel Stein and Lockwood Kipling. The latter's appraisal referred to a similar, though smaller and less intact Bodhisatva from Takht-i-Bahi already in the museum's collection. This was likely the fragmented image published in Grünwedel & Burgess 1901: 185, ill. 131 (IC 23860; I 441), which is not a 'pensive' specimen. It may have been erroneously attributed to this site, though, as the accession entry of 1890 lists the provenance as "Jamalgarhi".

14 Cf. her first letter, dated 13 August 1910.

15 In fact, a question mark was added in the original acquisition entry and the doubt was expressed in the caption as well, using the word 'allegedly' in German (Le Coq 1922: 19). I am grateful to Ms Ines Buschmann for providing a scan of the entry.

up the two high-quality stelae with objects excavated at Takht-i-Bahi in 1871. This was the first official excavation at the site, carried out under the supervision of Sergeant F. H. Wilcher, assisted by a detachment of the Bengal Sappers and Miners, namely, members of the armed forces trained for heavy, groundbreaking work. The finds consisted of 165 objects, specified as images of Buddhas and Bodhisatvas,[16] which had been stored in the Public Works Department's inspection bungalow at Hoti Mardan after the excavation, where they remained until 1875,[17] although they must have been destined for the Lahore Museum right from the beginning.[18] The two impressive artworks were very probably selected there by George R. Elsmie, then Additional Commissioner, sometime in 1874,[19] formally handing them over to his wife, as an asset that could be monetised in case she would survive him. In support of this, there is a short comment on the stored works of art in Elsmie's autobiography, of 28 January 1873: "The collection of Buddhist sculptures excavated from the old mounds in the neighbourhood [of Mardan] is very interesting".[20] We can be relatively sure about the archaeological context now. However, the 1871 excavation was performed on a thoroughly disturbed site, as F. H. Wilcher stated that none of the objects were found in situ, in his short report published in 1874.[21] A useful plan of the architectural remains, which formed the basis of later site plans of the Takht-i-Bahi hill monastery, accompanied the report, though no drawings or photographs of the finds were made.[22]

16 Errington 1987: 331–332, 437; Errington 2022: 2, 29.

17 Errington 1987: 154, "The whole of the sculptures were removed [...] to the PWD bungalow at Hoti Mardan", which obviously happened in 1871. Regarding their final transfer to Lahore, Elizabeth Errington comments, in her email of 6 April 2022: "His [Lockwood Kipling's] appointment as head of the Museum [in Lahore] in 1875 coincided with the arrival of the finds excavated at Takht-i-Bahi in 1871 and Jamalgarhi in 1873, which were the first major official contributions to the collection".

18 Although Peshawar is closer to Takht-i-Bahi than Lahore, there was no museum with an official status yet, in the former location.

19 Elizabeth Errington, in her email of 6 April 2022, explains that "it was standard practice from the 1850s until the end of the 19th century and even later, for officials and officers responsible for the excavated material, to select sculptures from the excavated sites for themselves, before the sculptures were sent off to the Lahore Museum".

20 Elsmie 1908: 177. The following sentence runs: "The Muhammadans hereabouts are such iconoclasts that even the coolies chip the figures as they dig them [i.e, the statues] up."

21 Wilcher 1874.

22 D. B. Spooner (1911: 135), who excavated at Takht-i-Bahi during two campaigns, 1907–08 and 1908–09, put it that "he [Wilcher] appears to have dug merely enough to enable him to draw up the plan in question, for even in certain places where one would infer had been cleared thoroughly, sculptures were found in large numbers lying obviously as they had fallen". Cf. Errington 2022: 2.

Description of the stele

With about one quarter of its height broken off at the bottom, the figure of the Bodhisatva looks stouter than it would have appeared when complete in the past (**Figs. 1, 2**). Neither the overall shape, nor the dress or ornaments present any salient features as such. A conspicuous trait, however, is the slightly awkward tilt of the head to the proper right side and the extended index finger of the right hand touching the turban just behind a rosette through the centre of which a chain is passing. This 'awkward' impression is caused by the relatively strong inclination of the head contrasting with an otherwise straight back and shoulders, so that it appears almost forced. Further, an impressively large nimbus characterises the portrayed figure. It is placed in such a way that the Bodhisatva's right hand is accommodated within its circumference.

His squarish face with nearly-shut, elongated eyes, the well-shaped nose and small mouth separated by a slightly undulating moustache, has a central, protruding mark corresponding to the Buddha's *ūrṇā*. Curly hair is framing the face on both sides, and the Bodhisatva wears heavy earrings, with the preserved one showing parallel rows of pearls. His richly adorned turban has two superimposed central elements, probably gemstones, and culminates in a fan-shaped crest falling back over the central portion of the head, which is covered by ornamental bands. Further, a massive chain is suspended by the uppermost of the central elements, passing through symmetrically placed lateral rosettes. A heavy, long necklace, also provided with a central jewel, falls over a precious collar, encrusted with jewels, in its turn superimposing two more chains passing over the left shoulder. The thicker one is falling over the right arm, just below the shoulder, while the other is suspending several neatly aligned amulet containers. Finally, there are upper arm ornaments, of which only a small portion is visible on the bare right arm, and two wristlets on each arm. The clothing of the upper part of the body is a shawl, draped over both his arms. It is wound around the upper left arm in a specific manner for keeping it in place, which has been rendered very neatly. The backrest of the throne remains hidden from sight, apart from mere traces on both sides. A frieze of lotus petals forming its top portion is visible

Fig. 4 a&b *Two mourning female servants from an Attic family tomb, Menidi (Greece), 330/320 BCE, marble, Antikensammlung, Berlin; a: Inv. no. Sk 499, 102 x 49 x 75 cm; b: Inv. no. Sk 498, 100 x 41 x 67 cm © Staatliche Museen zu Berlin, Antikensammlung / Foto: Universität zu Köln, Archäologisches Institut, CoDArchLab, 10440_FA-SPerg-000277-01_Gisela Geng; CoDArchLab, 104038_FA-SPerg-000278-01_Gisela Geng*

on the proper left side. The Bodhisatva's legs are clearly held asymmetrically, with the right knee supporting the right elbow, so that the index finger of that hand reaches the lower portion of the turban.

The only attribute is held in the Bodhisatva's left hand. It had not been identified by 1922, when Le Coq's publication came out.[23] Meanwhile, we can be sure about reading it as an unusually small garland, or wreath. Objects of this overall type are ubiquitous in Buddhist art, with their artistic antecedents to be looked for in ancient Mediterranean art.[24] In this case of a rather common design, I suggest it is composed of flower petals neatly wrapped and held together by knotted threads.

Cross-reception with regard to classical Greek mourners?

A less researched field is the exploration of possibly interrelated receptions concerning exhibits presented in different venues belonging to a major cultural centre, however, where they would be frequented by basically the same group of visitors. In the present case, a certain emotional response to a pair of rare and exquisite marble sculptures of mourning female servants, likely slaves, from late classical Greece, c. 330/320 BCE (**Fig. 4**),[25] could have impacted the way in which the Bodhisatva was perceived. These remarkable images in the round were acquired for the antique collection at *Altes Museum*, Berlin, in 1884 and became known as one of the highlights of the permanent exhibition, according to Berlin travel guides of 1891 and 1922.[26] The emotional response to these figures might have resembled, in certain respects, the visitors' reaction to the Elsmie Bodhisatva, with the latter being an image from a largely unknown cultural background, however. The main feature linking the Greek statues with the Elsmie Bodhisatva would have been the inclined head, with one hand drawn close to it, though the actual hand posture differs. In addition, the Bodhisatva's nearly closed eyelids, which are approximated by one of the Greek sculptures (**Fig. 4a**), might have enhanced the assumed expression of suffering, or mourning. The fact that many other displayed images from Gandhāra were sharing the feature of the 'drooping eyelids' could have been neglected by those who had felt a spontaneous emotional response to this particular artwork, triggered by a specific set of properties, basically comparable to those of the ancient Greek mourners. However, the sentiment of 'mourning' with its usual implications cannot be expected to arise in a Bodhisatva. It would be more appropriate to think of him as engaged in an analytical consideration, or 'contemplation', though even such readings are external ascriptions, in the absence of any pertinent textual hints. Intriguingly,

23 Le Coq 1922: 19.

24 Garlands and wreaths should ideally be differentiated. If we suppose that a wreath is worn on someone's head, this is in place here, as there are a few images of Bodhisatvas wearing this long, pliable variant (cf. n. 53). For a study of garlands and wreaths in other contexts of Gandhāran art, see Stoye 2007.

25 Cf. Schwarzmaier & Scholl 2019: 118–122, cat. nos. 65 & 66.

26 Berlin 1891: 93; Berlin 1922: 102.

the means themselves, by which the – widely perceived – contemplative expression has been achieved for the Elsmie Bodhisatva, are most probably derived from ancient Mediterranean art.

Similar representations

Even if I shall argue, further down below, that the pointing gesture is a case of isolated appropriation of a likely originally imperial-Roman iconographic motif, it appears to be well-rooted in Gandhāran art, as becomes apparent in its numerous variants and settings. More correctly, the so-called 'pensive' type of Bodhisatva forms part of a larger typological cluster comprising other shades of emotional states. Thus, an interesting case of a character depicted in a 'pensive' attitude, here expressing disappointment and perhaps, self-accusation, is Māra, the historical Buddha's antagonist, who would be blaming himself after unsuccessfully attempting to impede the Buddha's Enlightenment.[27]

Although there are numerous publications presenting and investigating 'pensive', or 'contemplative', Bodhisatvas,[28] it can be observed that the gesture of holding one hand close to the head, touching it with one finger, has not yet been studied specifically. Unfortunately, space is lacking for a fully adequate discussion and illustration of all identified pieces of evidence on which my conclusions are based. The conspicuous gesture of the hand has often been obliterated by the breakage of the respective forearm, hand, or finger, a problem that even includes narrative reliefs, so that the original evidence has been substantially, and perhaps unproportionally, reduced by the vagaries of history.[29] One of the results of my survey is that the overall type, as far as it can be ascertained, remains relatively rare, though several variants concerning the position of the hand, and extended finger, do exist. Intriguingly, the Elsmie Bodhisatva preserves certain idiosyncrasies singling him out. In this respect, the relatively flat execution of forms and the abrupt, and thus, slightly awkward tilt of the head to the Bodhisatva's right appear to me as indicators.

A few significant differences can be made out while comparing the stele to its most important analogue, another Pensive Bodhisatva from Takht-i-Bahi, on display in the Peshawar Museum (**Fig. 5**). The label refers to the excavation by the American archaeologist D. B. Spooner of 1908–09.[30] It is carved in higher relief, even comprising undercut portions like the right upper arm. The forearm is, unfortunately, broken off just beyond the elbow. As one of the significant features, the garland, or wreath, is much larger and has a different surface structure revealing leaves, as in a laurel wreath. The male figure's torso and limbs are markedly slimmer. Other divergences can be discerned in the face. It appears to be without moustache, the overall shape of the eyes has an elegant curvature, and the nose and mouth seem to be merging, in the absence of a philtrum, that is, the natural space between them.[31] Interestingly, except for basically conforming contours, and even breakage, this slightly smaller effigy shows a different treatment of practically all details (turban, hair, ornaments,[32] etc.), so that one might even surmise that the artist had consciously created 'different solutions', while being aware of the other, probably earlier, piece. This must remain a hypothesis, however. Interestingly, the inclination of the head is here similarly pronounced, if not even slighty stronger. Another significant element of the Bodhisatva at Peshawar is the large visible portion of the throne, with the two corner ornaments of the backrest representing a variant of the quatrefoil motif that occurs frequently in Gandhāra (cf. the centrepiece of the 'collar' ornament in **Fig. 10**)[33].

27 Quagliotti 1996a.

28 E.g., Lee 1993; Quagliotti 1996, 1996a, and 2000. The latter author included a critique of the former.

29 During the course of this study, I decided not to discuss any examples kept in Japan, as there might be instances of restorations, which at least in some cases may not express the original concept. This decision of mine should not reflect negatively on Japanese collections in general. It is a precautionary measure, particularly, as the long distance precludes me from visiting and taking a first-hand look.

30 There is no proper report on the works carried out in 1908–09. Only one paragraph was included in Vogel 1912: 3. If the assignment of the stele to this campaign is correct, then it implies that it was found "southeast of the court of the many little stūpas, [...] in what now appear to have been originally chapels" (*ibid.*).

31 This strange tendency of reducing the space between nose and mouth (*philtrum*), sometimes omitting it altogether, can be observed in a number of instances, e.g. in a stele that was likewise housed in the Berlin Museum für Völkerkunde and was relocated after World War II, namely, IC 37058 (Le Coq 1922: 19; Taf. 2; Dreyer et al. 2002: 40; Rhi 2018: 287, fig. 17).

32 The Pensive Bodhisatva from Takht-i-Bahi kept in the Peshawar Museum is missing the upper arm ornament on his right arm, whereas on his left side, an angular, oblong shape is clearly visible through the drapery. It is a very rare case of asymmetry in this respect.

33 For further examples of the quatrefoil motif appearing in jewellery, with a certain degree of variation, see Tissot 1985: pl. 31, 1; pl. 33, 5, 8, 9; pl. 34, 1; figs. 213, 224 a & b.

A further analogue comes from Loriyan Tangai (**Fig. 6**), and this image was fortunately recorded on site in a late 19th-century photograph of an impressive assemblage of sculptural remains.[34] It differs from the two figures described so far and functions more like an image in the round, exhibiting naturally-shaped limbs. In this case, the tilt of the head is skilfully rendered by a slight deviation from the plumb line. Thereby, it represents a clear typological advancement over the former two examples, though it is difficult to say whether it may indeed be significantly later, due to the overall difficulties in periodicising Gandhāran art. Regrettably, again, the right arm is broken beyond the elbow, so that the position of the hand cannot be ascertained. Other signs of a further development may be traced in the voluminously rendered turban and the wisps of hair ending in fine undulating curls (both for moustache and scalp hair). The large, plain nimbus of the two former images (**Figs. 1** and **5**) similarly occurs with the Loriyan Tangai Bodhisatva (**Fig. 6**). Singular features in this connection are: his right leg fully crossing the trunk and placed horizontally, with the ankle and foot supported by the left knee. Further specific features are the broad throne without backrest, with massive lathe-turned legs, and drapery in between, and a footstool placed in front, where an empty sandal appears on the proper right side, beside the sandalled left foot. His attribute is a large budding lotus flower drooping downwards.

Two further similar and well-preserved examples are only discussed here, as their illustrations are easily accessible. The third one in the sequence, which belongs to the Ashmolean Museum in Oxford, is quite small, with a height of 25.5 cm. It is a charming rendering of the 'pensive' type, where the middle finger of the right hand, instead of the index finger, touches the forehead just below the turban.[35] In this case, the right foot has been pulled up on the seat's front edge, where it rests as if suspended by the fanning centre portion of the Bodhisatva's upper garment (generally referred to as *uttarīya*).[36] The left hand is

Fig. 5 'Pensive Bodhisatva', Takht-i-Bahi (Pakistan), c. 3rd century, schist, 56 x 33 cm, Peshawar Museum (Pakistan). © Christian Luczanits

holding a large, half-open lotus bud. The almost childlike facial features combined with small hands and feet have a number of analogues in Gandhāran art, conforming as well to the smaller size, though not to the 'pensive' type, with one example datable to the third century, by stratigraphical evidence from Barikot, Swat Valley.[37] Because of their small sizes, such images could have been transported quite easily, and thus, the findspot may not be the place where they were created.

The fourth comparandum belongs to the Los Angeles County Museum of Art.[38] It has a few unusual traits, which could speak for a less-studied substyle. With its height of 59 cm, it is smaller than the Elsmie stele, particularly, when considering that the latter is incomplete. Intriguingly, it exhibits another variant of 'childlike' proportions in that the head is depicted too large compared to the rest of the body. This is quite a an unexpected fea-

34 Luczanits 2008: 22, fig. 5. A cut-out of this important photograph has been published in Theuns-de Boer 2008: fig. 3; by Alexander E. Caddy, 1890s (probably, 1896), Indian Museum List 1042, albumen print, 24 x 28.5 cm. Album 2, p. 86. The sculpture that was later assigned the acc. no. 4993 appears in the bottom row, as the second image from the left with its face intact.

35 See https://collections.ashmolean.org/object/354764 (acc. no. EAOS.26.c); Jongeward 2019: frontispiece & 113, cat. no. 79.

36 For the use of the terms *uttarīya* (shawl) and *paridhāna* ('loincloth') in secondary literature, see Tissot 1985: 70–71; pl. XXIV, with examples.

37 Luczanits 2008: 338, cat. no. 254 (preaching Bodhisatva).

38 https://collections.lacma.org/node/175807 (acc. no. AC1994.8.1).

Fig. 6 'Pensive Bodhisatva', Loriyan Tangai (Pakistan), c. 3rd century, schist, 71.5 x 42 x 17 cm, inv. no. 4993, Indian Museum, Kolkata © Reinhard Neumann

ture, along with the rather unadorned turban, the unusual decoration of the nimbus, three parallel patches of cascading cloth, and a somewhat casually held drooping flower bud. His right index finger touches his right eyebrow just above the apex. The wicker seat, which is similarly seen with other examples of the overall type, is very small in proportion. The figure's right leg is crossing the body horizontally, as in the case of Loriyan Tangai (**Fig. 6**).

An important fact that has to be pointed out in this connection is a certain, though still largely unclear, relationship with the biographic episode of the historical Bodhisatva's First Meditation, happening when he was still young and spontaneously attained a powerful meditative state. It does not form part of the major life events of Buddha Śākyamuni, and references in Buddhist scriptures are not uniform.[39] To make things more complicated, this is not the only event in the historical Buddha's life which has been visualised involving a 'pensive' aspect.[40]

A characteristic marker of the Bodhisatva's First Meditation is the rose-apple tree (*jambu*) that shaded him, and therefore, it is assumed that representations without this essential detail do not qualify to be considered as depicting this scene. Unfortunately, many narrative reliefs featuring this characteristic figure, in the majority of cases with one leg crossing just above the pendant leg, and where we can make out the tree (not always shown correctly as a *jambu*), survive only in a damaged form.[41] What further complicates the overall situation is the fact that the First Meditation can be alternatively shown as a Bodhisatva seated in the usual cross-legged posture (*vajraparyaṅka*), with both hands resting in the lap, in *dhyānamudrā*. In these cases, certain indicators, often a ploughman with two horses, would be present.

Examples of a larger, basically one-figure type of stele, and thus, from a presumably non-narrative context, significantly resembling the format under discussion, are extremely rare. A fragmented Bodhisatva stele to be mentioned in this respect comes from Sanghao, c. 30 km northeast of Takht-i-Bahi.[42] Quite intriguingly, the extended overlong index finger of his right hand touches the lateral portion of his face roughly at the level of his mouth, with the thumb of his right hand bent upwards in a peculiar manner. There remains hardly any doubt that this is a visualisation of the historical Bodhisatva's First Meditation, particularly, because the tree sorrounding the halo could well be a *jambu*. A miniature tree god on the viewer's right is worshipping him. Notably, the Bodhisatva's torso, neck and head are perfectly straight, and in this do not resemble the Bodhisatva under discussion.[43]

39 Schlingloff 1987; Quagliotti 1996: 102–106.

40 Quagliotti has assembled particularly important evidence in this respect. One of her new findings is the depiction of a 'pensive' moment before the Great Renunciation, in five instances (1996: 102, and n. 9).

41 A rare exception is illustrated in Quagliotti 1996: 107, fig. 9.

42 Luczanits 2008: 275, cat. no. 201.

43 Intriguingly, a few basically coeval figures, though without attributes, are known from Mathuran art, which likewise show a perfectly straight posture, and similarly, touch the lower portion of their face with their fingers: Czuma 1985: 77–79, cat. 41, referred to as "Avalokiteśvara".

Possible antecedents of the Gandhāran pointing gesture as seen at Takht-i-Bahi

It will be argued that a transfer of the conspicuous feature of the pointing gesture, most often, with the index finger extended, from ancient Roman art had taken place in the early centuries CE, in the form of an inspirational adoption, and customisation, on the Gandhāran side.[44] The transfer would have happened in different stages, which resulted in certain asynchronisms between imperial Roman and Gandhāran art, particularly, as my study suggests a mediating role performed by Palmyra, located in an oasis in the Roman province of Syria, and an ancient trading hub. Here, the sculptural art of funerary reliefs integrated in certain types of architecture had flourished from about the second half of the 1st century CE.[45] Both in Palmyra, which formed part of the Roman province of Syria for an extended period, and closer to the capital of the Roman empire, funerary monuments are indeed exhibiting pointers to an ancient linkage between the three centres forming cultural spheres of their own.

Starting from the early imperial period, an exemplary case can be identified in the funerary relief of Lucius Vibius, his wife Vecilia, and their son (**Fig. 7**), from Cesano, located to the north of Rome. The impressive panel introduces three members of a family, with their names inscribed below. The rendering of the portraits is strictly frontal, and there are only few details in the representation. A single hand per person has been added for the adults, the right hand for the man, and the left hand for the woman. The former hand is clearly oversized. In Vecilia's case, both her arms are wrapped in the drapery of her cloak (*palla*) that also covers her head. As an important detail that has to be noted for comparison, her left hand with the index finger extended to touch the lower part of her cheek, clutches a portion of the cloth. Thus, her hand performing the 'pointing gesture' is nearly on all sides framed by cloth. Richard Brilliant comments on this depiction: "The linear treatment of the drapery, not yet fully matured as a compositional device, is keyed to the gestures of husband and wife [with the latter] set in a typical attitude of reflection and virtue".[46] These shades of meaning can be spontaneously felt on seeing Vecilia's portrait even nowadays. At the same time, the gesturally expressed notion of *pudicitia* (Lat. modesty, chastity, purity), is clearly a cultural convention of her time.[47] Pudicitia was also known as a personification of the well-behaved wife, and a specific cult surrounded her. The gesture under discussion originally refers to the correct handling of the veil-like portions of Roman women's clothing and may be reduced to grasping the hem with a simple, but graceful posture of the hand not necessarily touching the face.[48]

Fig. 7 Tomb relief of Lucius Vibius, his wife Vecilia Hilara, and son Felicio Felix, Cesano (Italy), mid-Augustan, 20/10 BCE, marble, 75 x 94.5 x 22 cm, Musei Vaticani, Rome, inv. no. 2109 © Forschungsarchiv für Antike Plastik am Archäologischen Institut der Universität zu Köln, Neg.-Nr.: Foto Oehler 33/1953/8

44 The other fingers of the respective hand are bent. During future studies, details like the exact delineation of the hand and fingers should be analysed.

45 See Heyn 2010, and referred publications. (For reasons of space, references have been kept to a minimum here.)

46 Brilliant 1963: 49.

47 Cf. Stewart 2003: 94, fig. 12. This example dates to c. late first century CE.

48 As an example for the veil-like cloth being held on both sides, the lavish mausoleum of the Haterii of the early 2nd century CE (c. 120 CE) shall be referred to. The bust of the female tomb owner

My argument shall be taken geographically further, to the stone sculpture of Palmyra. A huge number of funerary reliefs and an impressive and varied cemetery architecture had flourished in this ancient trading hub, until its downfall in the late third century. I have chosen an example that highlights another aspect of the cult of the dead, namely, the funerary banquet (**Fig. 8**). In this case, a sibling couple appears on scene, as they are reclining, supported by cushions to their left side. The woman's full body is visible, and an overall similarity with the attitude and dress of Vecilia in the earlier example becomes apparent. The head of the Palmyrene woman is covered in a similar manner, and her hand posture is quite comparable, too, while somewhat differently, her index finger touches another portion of the face, just above the left eyebrow. The attitude of well-to-do Palmyrenes exhibiting their rich jewellery clearly stands in contrast to the modesty of the Vibius family in ancient Italy. Two more features in this Palmyrene panel that can indeed be compared with their distant analogues in Gandhāra are the six-petalled stylised flowers, with one adorning the centre of the wreath on the man's head, while two others appear symmetrically on the curtain behind him (*dorsalium*); the second one is the quatrefoil with pointed tips recurring on the motif-repeat fabric below, while a variant of it adorns the centre of the woman's diadem.

Fig. 8 Funerary relief depicting a small banquet scene, hypogeum of Ta'ai, Palmyra (Tadmur, Syria), c. second half of 2nd century, limestone, 55 x 83.4 cm, National Museum, Damascus, inv. no. 18802 © akg-images / Erich Lessing

In Palmyra, there are many more funerary reliefs with comparable features, and the 'pointing gesture', with certain variants, is well-established in the repertoire. While exploring the relationship between the gesture as encountered in the Roman heartland vis-à-vis Palmyra, Maura Heyn is calling for a differentiated assessment: "this raised-arm gesture is similar to the *pudicitia* gesture in Rome, but it is not clear if it had similar connotations of modesty and fidelity in Palmyra".[49] In our context, the semantic aspect is not that essential, for the time being, as it is presumed that in Gandhāra, matters are again much different, not the least because the overall frame is Buddhist, the setting is not funerary (in the narrow sense), and the protagonists are all male.

It has been revealing to ascertain that the western part of Gandhāra, i.e. the Kapisa region, might have been a virtual hothouse regarding the use of the pointing gesture in sculptural art. The evidence adduced would be even more meaningful if chronological questions could be better addressed. However, the observation of different ways of the feature's application and its visual emphasis, achieved by a certain morphological simplification and standardisation, speak for themselves. The image that illustrates best the possibility of a multi-layered semantic fabric woven around it, and difficult to assess, is the enigmatic Bodhisatva from Shotorak seated on a reclining elephant, under an unspecified tree (**Fig. 9**).

appears in the tympanum of a temple-shaped tomb shown in relief (Sinn & Freyberger 1996: Taf. 12). She is framed by four- and five-petalled flowers, which will be used for comparison below.

49 Heyn 2010: 635.

Published first in the 1942 report by Jacques Meunié, it was again evaluated by the late Anna Maria Quagliotti, who identified the image as the historical Bodhisatva's First Meditation.[50] Apart from the unique feature of a Bodhisatva seated on a reclining elephant, further unusual traits are: behind and above the left hand displaying the 'pointing gesture', a flat version of Indra's thunderbolt (*vajra*) might be 'floating', and there are flames emerging from the entire left side of the body. The former feature might indicate a 'syncretic' concept of merging the Bodhisatva with aspects of Indra, or Śakra.[51] However, what should be noted foremost from this occurrence is the 'pointing gesture' carried out with the left hand.

Three more striking examples, showing the Buddha himself with this gesture, and that, with the respective hand standing out for its size, have been analysed by Katsumi Tanabe.[52] Surprisingly, two of these instances form part of one and the same panel, where the Buddha appears twice, once seated and once standing. At the same time, these altogether three figures discussed by him are the first examples in this short survey carrying out the pointing gesture with the right hand, in the same manner as displayed by the Elsmie Bodhisatva. Gestures of the *pudicitia* type in Palmyrene funerary art were exhibited with either the left or the right hand. It is clear, however, that the preference was laid on the right hand side in Gandhāra, with some exceptions (see also below).[53]

Fig. 9 First Meditation of Bodhisatva Śākyamuni (?), Shotorak (Afghanistan), c. 3rd century, schist, 35 x 13 cm, Musée Guimet, Paris, inv. no. MG21160 © bpk / RMN – Grand Palais / image musée Guimet

In order to support my observation that certain parts of the morphological repertoire of ancient Roman as well as, specifically, Palmyrene funerary art were adopted in Gandhāra, a similar instance of transfer will be briefly introduced. Flowers, including the ubiquitous lotus, form an important part of the morphological repository of Gandhāran sculptural art. Apart from the lotus serving as a frequent attribute, taking an altogether wide range of shapes, standardised blossom motifs seen in top view, are extremely frequent, but yet, their potential for establishing links between different schools of art has been overlooked. Among these, four-, five- and six-petalled forms of rosettes appear particularly often, while seven- and eight-petalled rosettes are not unknown. The Elsmie Bodhisatva exhibits two six-petalled flowers, symmetrically arranged on his turban, through the centres of which a decorative chain passes, concealing one of the petals (**Fig. 1**). The Pensive Bodhisatva image from Loriyan Tangai likewise has the same kind of rosette, not connected by a chain, however (**Fig. 6**). While tracing the related flower motifs back to their likely Mediterranean origins, it is revealing to note that both the five- and six-petalled blossoms (cinquefoil and hexafoil) are often seen in imperial Roman funerary art.[54] Five- and six-petalled flowers are as well met with in Palmyra, in important loci within the relief panels,[55] and this can be stated for Gandhāra, too.[56] It is particularly noteworthy that such a flower motif often occupies the central por-

50 Quagliotti 1996: 104–105.

51 If so, it might be compared with a rare case of depicting a Bodhisatva, probably of the 'pensive' type, with the paraphernalia of the Moon god, as identified by Quagliotti (2000: 1144–1148).

52 Tanabe 2012: 190–191, figs. 3–6; 198, fig. 9.

53 Bodhisatva images originally with their left hands held close to their face, are unfortunately, mostly damaged. For two examples at Musée Guimet, Paris, see Geoffroy-Schneiter (2001: fig. [12]; left arm broken above elbow, garland or wreath wrapped twice around the head), and Luczanits (2008: 247, fig. 7; cf. also Rhi 2018: fig. 24; head and large parts of left arm missing, right hand holding a small book).

54 Boschung 1987: Taf. 1–6 (multiple examples).

55 For the hexafoil, see my Fig. 8; for the cinquefoil, see Ingholt 1954: figs. 4 (= Heyn 2010: fig. 10) & 6.

56 E.g., Errington 2022: 27, fig. 23, C3/C12 (Takht-i-Bahi, cinquefoil in the apex); 30, fig. 26, S4. The former item compares well with Luczanits 2008: 230, cat. no. 174, which has a frieze of cinquefoils along the ogee arch.

tion of a wreath, seen frontally, which suggests that it would have functioned like a clasp (**Fig. 8**, right). In such a ritually vulnerable and accentuated position it betrays its extraordinary role which must have included auspicious and apotropaic aspects. The most astonishing evidence I could identify so far is the virtually identical shape of a wreath with a central cinquefoil motif depicted on a Roman grave altar (Vespasianic, 69–79 CE) and on the large complex stele from Muhammad Nari (see also below), where the wreath is suspended over the central Buddha's head.[57] A sole example for the extensive usage of the five-petalled rosette in Gandhāra is a long-attested image of a standing Bodhisatva in the Metropolitan Museum of Art, New York (**Fig. 10**). Four cinquefoil motifs are on the socle, while another pair adorns the upper arm ornaments, with only the one on the right arm visible. Intriguingly, the astragal motif, another clearly 'western' design, has been applied on the sandal straps, while his precious collar's central element is a quatrefoil, as mentioned above.

Fig. 10 Standing Bodhisatva of the Maitreya type, Gandhāra, c. 2nd/3rd century, schist, 80.7 x 29 x 15 cm, Metropolitan Museum of Art, New York, acc. no. 13.96.17 © Metropolitan Museum of Art, NYC, Public Domain

Possible pointers to a conceptual frame, name, and date

It is fascinating, though also puzzling, to find the overall type under discussion at times participating in larger compositional arrangements, either of the 'triad' type, comprising three juxtaposed main characters, or belonging to the so-called 'complex stelae', with the larger ones featuring an impressive assembly of various figural elements. Both categories have, in recent years, received much scholarly attention.[58] In both cases – mostly – Bodhisatvas are grouped around a central Buddha shown in the teaching attitude (*dharmacakrapravartanamudrā*). Both in triadic representations and in complex stelae, the presence of members of the Pensive Bodhisatva type is not compulsory, though, when these occur, a highly specific content could possibly be encoded here, relating to aspects of liberation on the Buddhist path.[59]

The largest among several stelae that were recovered from Muhammad Nari, located to the west of Takht-i-Bahi, is one of the best examples for symmetrically conceived 'pensive' participants, forming almost perfect mirror images of each other (for the one on the viewer's right, see **Fig. 11**).[60] The symmetric pair appears on the topmost level. The 'doubling' should convince everyone of the fact that a 'pensive' character is as such not singular. The fact that their attributes differ in those cases, exhibiting the already noted alternation of a wreath/garland and a lotus of various shapes,[61] may be only a minor adjustment, concealing the fact that the 'pensive' character as such is not a separate individual, but more of a morphological template.

The other example provided here shows the proper left side of the well-known fragmented triad kept in the Ringling Museum, Sarasota, Fl. (**Fig. 12**). There is hardly any doubt that a symmetrically arranged 'pensive' counterpart was depicted on the proper right side.[62] This panel has been noted for carrying an important inscription. If we compare the Sarasota Pensive Bodhisatva with the right one seen at Muhammad Nari (**Fig. 11**), there are quite a few minor differences concerning the tilt of the head, the position of the right leg, the presence or absence of sandals, and even the attributes. How-

57 Boschung 1987: Taf. 3, 88; Luczanits 2008: 276, cat. no. 204; Harrison & Luczanits 2012: 197, fig. 1.

58 For triads, see Miyaji 2022 and the author's previous studies referred to; for complex stelae, see Harrison & Luczanits 2012.

59 Harrison & Luczanits 2012: 112.

60 For the symmetric counterpart and the full view of the stele, see Luczanits 2008: 256, fig. 3; 276, cat. no. 204; for the full view and other close-ups, see Harrison & Luczanits 2012: 197, fig. 1; 199, figs. 3–4.

61 Schmidt (2005) postulates that both major variants, regarding the attribute, are forms of Avalokiteśvara.

62 Cf. Harrison & Luczanits 2012: 207, fig. 17 (a frequently published triad from Loriyan Tangai).

ever, their style and overall presentation render them basically coeval, in my view. The inscription of the Sarasota panel had been taken as referring to Amitābha, until 20 years ago, when Salomon and Schopen refuted this interpretation, which was widely accepted.[63] The same inscription contains the word "*oloiśpare*", which could be equivalent to "Avalok[it]eśvara".[64] This reading is still perpetuated by some authors, after Salomon and Schopen had argued against it, and that with good reasons, in my view.[65] Not only in order to prevent addressing too many research questions simultaneously, it should be wise to follow the example of Juhyung Rhi, who has advocated a balanced approach that refrains from assigning names to Bodhisatvas wherever a relatively high degree of typological variation is apparent.[66] A cautious approach is also advisable, because the still advancing textual research sometimes produces quite unexpected results,[67] suggesting that our knowledge of the developments that led to early Mahāyāna Buddhist concepts may yet be incomplete.

Fig. 11 'Pensive Bodhisatva', detail of a large complex stele (above, right), Muhammad Nari (Pakistan), c. 3rd century, light grey schist, height: c. 18.3 cm (complete height: 119 cm), Lahore Museum, inv. no. G-155 © Christian Luczanits

Another inscription seen on a triadic panel contains a rare date.[68] An obstacle has to be overcome here, since the Kuṣāṇa convention of conveying historical dates does not allow proceeding beyond one hundred. Juhyung Rhi's interpretation of the given date of „Year 5" as c. 232 is convincing in this respect. Thus, with the triad formerly prefixed with "De Marteau", or "Brussels", involving the usual seated preaching Buddha and two laterally standing Bodhisatvas, we have proceeded well into the 3rd century, though not beyond the first half. Since the Elsmie Bodhisatva comes stylistically quite close to the "Year 5" panel and the production of triads and complex stelae did not last for a long period of time, in my view, it may be dated to the 3rd century almost without doubt.

A last piece of evidence will be extracted from the rich and intricate evidence offered by the preaching Buddha configurations. One among several examples of complex stelae from Muhammad Nari published by Harrison and Luczanits can be compared to a fragment of a similar stele from Takht-i-Bahi, preserving a Pensive Bodhisatva.[69] In both cases, he is depicted as seated in a pavilion with a cruciform plan. This specific setting includes a standing worshipper on each side, and in the latter case, two more worshippers are squatting on the roof ridge. This clearly demonstrates that Takht-i-Bahi, located not far from Muhammad Nari, would have partaken in the same concepts, with these including the early Mahāyāna complex stelae. From this premise we can ultimately infer that the image under discussion is indeed a Mahāyāna Bodhisatva.

Concluding thoughts

Hopefully, I have been able to reasonably outline the likely geographical route for the transfer of the highly specific 'pointing (or deictic) gesture' from imperial Roman – in particular, funerary – art, through the ancient Syrian metropolis of Palmyra. The Palmyrene culture flourished during a period largely coinciding with the emergence and heyday of Gandhāran art in stone. The selective

63 Salomon & Schopen 2002.

64 See the entry https://gandhari.org/catalog?textID=222, with bibliography.

65 Salomon & Schopen 2002: 31. Miyaji (2022: 273, fig. 4, n. 15) has returned to the earlier held opinion recognising both Amitābha (centre, now viewer's left) and Avalokiteśvara (viewer's right).

66 Rhi 2018. The Elsmie stele is referred to just as "Bodhisattva" (Rhi 2018: 293, fig. 23), which is in order. With Maitreya, the future Buddha, matters may be different, as he appears to have conformed to a relatively well-delineated visual type early on.

67 Salomon (2018: 89) points out the mention of "the pure realm of an otherwise unknown Buddha Vipulaprabhāsa or Mahāprabha", recently found in a text from the Bajaur collection.

68 See Harrison & Luczanits 2012: 202, fig. 6; https://gandhari.org/catalog?itemID=206 (online entry). The panel is on loan to the Metropolitan Museum, New York.

69 For Takht-i-Bahi, see Tissot 1985: 158–159, pl. 3, 5. For Muhammad Nari, see Harrison & Luczanits 2012: 96–97; 204, fig. 10. It may be noted that, exceptionally, the 'pensive' figure of the right-hand version does not have a 'pensive' counterpart on the viewer's left, but a frontally facing one with legs crossing at the ankles.

adoption of certain elements on the latter side must have been a proactive choice, and not a merely passive or mechanical process.

Concerning the 'pointing gesture', it may be noted that it significantly occurs in certain ancient Roman funerary contexts, being somewhat reworked in Palmyra, where the funerary culture flourished and developed its own 'visual vocabulary'. It was performed with a straight back, neck and head, which has been as well observed in the Kapisa region of Afghanistan (**Fig. 9**), and it certainly did not express sadness or mourning but made an obviously 'mute' culturally encoded statement. As far as I can see, only in the heartland of Gandhāra was the extended index finger combined with an inclination of the head. A similar tilt, though without the 'pointing gesture', likewise occurs on ancient Mediterranean sculpture, as the two statues from classical Greece have demonstrated (**Fig. 4**), with the underlying emotional content of sadness and related shades. The supposedly Gandhāran innovation of combining the pointing finger with a tilted head resulted in an even more suggestive expression. Figures exhibiting this attitude apparently became suitable participants in certain types of relief panels centring on a preaching Buddha, likely explicating early Mahāyāna concepts, in ways not yet grasped by us. The 'duplication' occurring in this context proved so successful that it was adopted in Central Asia and the Far East.[70] Along this line, a rejoinder may now be offered to Le Coq's assertion of 1922 that the Elsmie Bodhisatva had formed part of a group.[71] One hundred years later, there is still no indication that such near life-sized stelae were indeed conceived to be combined with others in a meaningful way (although it cannot be ruled out either). What may be attested, however, is that the overall shape with an inclination to one side, dramatically highlighted by this compelling hand gesture, is intrinsically calling for a complement. And this is beautifully demonstrated by some of the triadic and complex stelae just discussed, and it also finds expression in the rare pair of Attic mourners (**Fig. 4**), though far removed in time and space.

Fig. 12 Preaching Buddha and 'Pensive Bodhisatva' (fragmented, inscribed triadic panel), Gandhāra (Pakistan), c. 3rd century, schist, 30.5 x 26 x 6.5 cm, Ringling Museum of Art, Sarasota (Fl., USA), MF94.8.5 © The John and Mable Ringling Museum of Art

Thus, in several respects, the stele under discussion has now revealed pieces of information it has been saving for a long time, thereby virtually approximating what we may regard as its 'true identity', shedding its former cognomen "Mourning Avalokiteśvara" in the process.

Acknowledgements

Let me express my gratitude to the concerned museum staff, both in Berlin and St Petersburg, and to the following individuals, for helping me with images and counsel: Dietrich Boschung (Köln), Elizabeth Errington (London), Frederik Grosser (Berlin), Christian Luczanits (London), and Rhiannon Paget (Sarasota).

70 E.g., Lee 1993: figs. 10 (Kizil); 26 (Yungang).
71 Le Coq 1922: 19 (Begleitfigur aus einer größeren Gruppe).

Bibliography

Berlin 1891 = *Berlin, Potsdam und Umgebungen* (1891) Berlin (Praktischer Wegweiser, Griebens Reise-Bibliothek, 6; 37th enlarged edition).

Berlin 1922 = *Berlin, Potsdam and Environs* (1922) Berlin (Practical Guide, Griebens Guide Books, 108a; 5th edition).

Berlin 1926 = *Vorläufiger Führer durch das Museum für Völkerkunde, Schausammlung* (1926). Berlin & Leipzig (18th edition).

Boschung, Dietrich (1987) *Antike Grabaltäre aus den Nekropolen Roms*. Bern (Acta Bernensia, 10).

Brilliant, Richard (1963) *Gesture and Rank in Roman Art: The Use of Gestures to Denote Status in Roman Sculpture and Coinage*. New Haven, Conn. (Memoirs of the Connecticut Academy of Arts and Sciences, 14).

Czuma, Stanislaw J. (1985) *Kushan Sculpture: Images from Early India*. Cleveland, Ohio.

Dreyer, Caren *et al.* (2002) *Verzeichnis seit 1945 vermisster Bestände der ehemaligen Indischen Abteilung des Museums für Völkerkunde, des heutigen Museums für Indische Kunst*. Berlin (Staatliche Museen zu Berlin, Dokumentation der Verluste, 3).

Elsmie, George Robert (1908) *Thirty-Five Years in the Punjab, 1858–1893*. Edinburgh.

Errington, Elizabeth (1987) *The Western Discovery of the Art of Gandhāra and the Finds of Jamālgarhī* (PhD Thesis). London.

—— (2022) Reconstructing Jamālgarhī and Appendix B: the archaeological record, 1848–1923. *The Rediscovery and Reception of Gandhāran Art*, eds. Wannaporn Rienjang, Peter Stewart. Oxford: 1–42.

Geoffroy-Schneiter, Bérénice (2001) *Gandhara: The Memory of Afghanistan*, New York.

Grünwedel, Albert & [revised and enlarged by] James Burgess (1901) *Buddhist Art in India*. London.

Harrison, Paul & Christian Luczanits (2012) New Light on (and from) the Muhammad Nari Stele. 浄土教に関する 特別国際シンポジウム *(Special International Symposium on Pure Land Buddhism)*. Kyoto (BARC International Symposium Series, 1): 69 –127; 197–207.

Heyn, Maura K. (2010) Gesture and Identity in the Funeral Art of Palmyra. *American Journal of Archaeology* (Boston, Mass.) 114.4: 631–661.

[Ingholt, Harald] (1954) *Palmyrene and Gandharan Sculpture (An Exhibition Illustrating the Cultural Interrelations Between the Parthian Empire and its Neighbors West and East, Palmyra and Gandhara)*. New Haven.

Jongeward, David (2019) *Buddhist Art of Gandhara in the Ashmolean Museum*. Oxford.

Le Coq, Albert von (1922) *Die buddhistische Spätantike in Mittelasien,* 1. Teil: *Die Plastik*. Berlin.

Lee, Junghee (1993) The Origins and Development of the Pensive Bodhisattva Images of Asia. *Artibus Asiae* (Zurich) 53.3–4: 311–357.

Luczanits, Christian, ed. (2008) *Gandhara: Das buddhistische Erbe Pakistans: Legenden, Klöster und Paradiese*. Mainz (Engl. edition, with identical pagination and catalogue nos.: *Gandhara, the Buddhist Heritage of Pakistan: Legends, Monasteries, and Paradise*).

Meunié, Jacques (1942) *Shotorak*. Paris (Mémoires de la délégation archéologique française en Afghanistan, 10).

Miyaji, Akira (2022) Aspects of Mahāyāna Buddhist Art in Gandhara: Focusing on the Iconography of Steles of the Triad Type and Emanation Type. *Connecting the Art, Literature, and Religion of South and Central Asia: Studies in Honour of Monika Zin*, eds. Ines Konczak-Nagel *et al.* New Delhi: 267–279.

Quagliotti, Anna Maria (1996) ‘Pensive’ Bodhisattvas on ‘Narrative’ Gandharan Reliefs: A Note on a Recent Study and Related Problems. *East and West* (Rome) 46: 97–115.

—— (1996a) Māra in a ‘Pensive’ Attitude in Buddhist Art. *Studies in Symbolism and Iconology* (Tokyo) 10: 10–29.

—— (2000) A Gandharan Bodhisattva with Sūrya on the Headdress and Related Problems. *South Asian Archaeology 1997: Proceedings of the Fourteenth International Conference of the European Association of South Asian Archaeologists*, Vol. 3, eds. Maurizio Taddei & Giuseppe De Marco. Rome: 1125–1154.

Rhi, Juhyung (2018) Looking for Mahāyāna Bodhisattvas: A Reflection on Visual Evidence in Early Indian Buddhism. *Setting Out on the Great Way: Essays on Early Mahāyāna Buddhism*, ed. Paul Harrison. Sheffield: 243–301.

Salomon, Richard (2018) *The Buddhist Literature of Ancient Gandhāra: An Introduction with Selected Translations*. Somerville, Mass.

Salomon, Richard & Gregory Schopen (2002) On an Alleged Reference to Amitābha in a Kharoṣṭhī Inscription on a Gandhāran Relief. *Journal of the International Association of Buddhist Studies* (Leuven) 25.1–2: 3–31.

SCHLINGLOFF, Dieter (1987) Die Meditation unter dem Jambu-Baum. *Wiener Zeitschrift für die Kunde Südasiens* (Wien) 31: 111–130.

SCHMIDT, Carolyn Woodford (2005) Evidence Suggesting the Simultaneous Development of Two Forms of Avalokiteśvara in Ancient Greater Gandhāra: A Preliminary Report. *South Asian Archaeology 2003: Proceedings of the Seventeenth International Conference of the European Association of South Asian Archaeologists*, eds. Ute Franke-Vogt & Hans-Joachim Weisshaar. Aachen: 403–410.

SCHNEIDER, Britta (2018) The beginning and development of Gandhāran collections in German public museums. *Buddhism and Gandhara: An Archaeology of Museum Collections*, ed. Himanshu Prabha Ray. London & New York: 213–231.

SCHWARZMAIER, Agnes & Andreas SCHOLL, ed. (2019) *Katalog der Skulpturen in der Antikensammlung der Staatlichen Museen zu Berlin*, Band 2, Teil 1: *Griechische Rundskulpturen bis zum Hochhellenismus*. Berlin.

SINN, Friederike & Klaus S. FREYBERGER (1996) *Katalog der Skulpturen*; Band 1: *Die Grabdenkmäler*; 2: *Die Ausstattung des Hateriergrabes*. Mainz (Monumenta artis Romanae, 24).

SPOONER, D. B. (1911) Excavations at Takht-i-Bāhī. *Archaeological Survey of India, Annual Report, 1907–08*. Calcutta: 132–148.

STEWART, Peter (2003) *Statues in Roman Society: Representation and Response*. Oxford.

STOYE, Martina (2007) *Serta Laurea* zu Ehren Buddhas – Zur gestreckten Lorbeerblattgirlande im Reliefdekor gandhārischer Stūpas. *Berliner Indologische Studien* (Berlin) 18: 241–318.

TANABE, Katsumi (2012) Iconographical Study of a limestone Buddhist relief unearthed in Northern Afghanistan: The Two Buddhas juxtaposed beside the Bodhi-Tree. *Parthica* (Pisa) 14: 189–201.

THEUNS-DE BOER, Gerda (2008) *A Vision of Splendour: Indian Heritage in the Photographs of Jean Philippe Vogel, 1901–1913*. Leiden.

TISSOT, Francine (1985) *Gandhâra*. Paris.

VOGEL, Jean Philippe (1912). Conservation. *Archaeological Survey of India, Annual Report, 1908–09*. Calcutta: 1–4.

WILCHER, F. H. (1874) Report on the Exploration of the Buddhist Ruins at Takht-i-Bai, January to April 1871, *Punjab Government Gazette* (Chandigarh), Supplement, 6th August 1874: 528–532 (reproduced in Errington 1987: 434–437).

Deutsche Zusammenfassung

Bei der Untersuchung der Objektgeschichte einer reliefierten Schieferstele, die sich von 1910 bis 1945 im Museum für Völkerkunde, Berlin, befunden hat (**Figs. 1–3**), konnten verschiedene Aspekte erhellt werden. Ihre Herkunft aus Takht-i-Bahi war beispielsweise nicht sicher belegt. Nun konnten Fakten herangezogen werden, die ihre Herkunft aus einer britischen Grabung an diesem bedeutenden Fundort von 1871 nahelegen. Kunsthistorisch betrachtet ist das Stück höchst aussagekräftig. Es konnte vorläufig nachgewiesen werden, dass die prägnante Zeigegeste auf die Grabkunst des Römischen Reichs der Kaiserzeit zurückgeht. Dort wurde sie insbesondere angewandt, um weibliche ‚Tugendhaftigkeit' bildlich auszudrücken. Ihr entsprechendes Auftreten in der Grabkunst Palmyras hat vermutlich als Vorbild für die Übernahme des Motivs in Gandhāra gedient. Da unter anderem spezifische Blütenornamente in gleicher Weise den Eingang in die Gandhāra-Kunst gefunden haben, lässt sich der Motivtransfer recht gut belegen. Das häufige Vorkommen dieses Figurentyps in komplexeren Darstellungen in Gandhāra und die dabei zu beobachtende Bildung eines symmetrischen Paars, mit den Köpfen zum Zentrum geneigt, legen es nahe, dass der Typus des sogenannten ‚nachdenklichen (oder kontemplativen) Bodhisatvas' wohl auch aus Gründen der Bildstrukturierung sehr beliebt war.

An Enigmatic Performer in Ajanta

Mercedes Tortorici

In a mural painting in Ajanta Cave I interpreted by Schlingloff as the depiction of the Sudhana story, there is a scene showing a male figure dressed in a peculiar long, striped tunic. Schlingloff identified this figure as a hunter mentioned in the Mūlasarvāstivāda version of the story. I argue here that the figure depicted is not a hunter, but rather a male dancer. The scene bears strong similarities with musical performances depicted in Bagh and Deogarh.

Musical performances are a frequent topic in Buddhist art. The Ajanta[1] paintings are no exception in this regard. Both female and male musical performers, i. e. dancers and musicians, are usually depicted as part of larger scenes, for example a king's coronation, or the Buddha's enlightment. On the left front corner of Ajanta's Cave I, a large mural painting was interpreted by Schlingloff as the depiction of the Sudhana story (Schlingloff: 1973, 2000/2013: vol. 1, 182ff.). One of the scenes of this mural depicts a traditional court scene, where a musical performance is taking place. Although some Ajanta musical depictions were considered in larger studies (Vatsyayan 1977: 307, 1982: 35–37, Zin 2004: 325, 333f.), the musical aspect of the scene discussed in this paper has never received particular attention in earlier scholarship.

Sudhana is a quite popular story among Buddhist narratives, included in several Buddhist story collections[2] and depicted in different Buddhist sites in Asia.[3] It is a romantic narrative about a prince called Sudhana and a beautiful *kinnarī*, who is captured by a hunter by means of a magical noose. In the Mūlasarvāstivāda version, a prequel narrates how the hunter gets this unfailing noose from a *nāga* king (Jaini 1966: 539; Schlingloff 1973: 157).

The Sudhana mural spreads partially on the left front and side walls of Ajanta Cave I. Schlingloff's interpretation of this painting is based on a scene depicted on the front wall of the cave, where the *kinnarī* is bathing with her female attendants. Prince Sudhana, who had been separated from his lover for a long time, dropped a signet ring, that she had previously asked an ascetic to give to him, into one of the vessels. While being bathed the ring fell into her lap, so she immediately knew her lover was in the palace.

Schlingloff also suggested that the prequel of the hunter arriving at the *nāga* palace to ask for the unfailing noose is depicted on the side wall of Ajanta Cave I (**Fig. 1, 2**). The *nāga* king, equipped with a serpent hood spread over his head, is sitting with his wife on the left side, while the hunter arrives at the palace to demand the magical noose. I argue here that the figure interpreted as the

1 Ajanta is the name of a Buddhist cave complex located in Maharashtra, India. The thirty caves at Ajanta, declared UNESCO World Heritage site in 1983, contain wall paintings from two phases. The earliest paintings in form of long friezes in Ajanta Caves IX and X are to be dated to the Sātavāhana period ca. 1st century BCE. The later paintings were painted in the 5th century CE. In this paper I will refer to the so-called Gupta art or Gupta style, that corresponds with Ajanta's second period. The Gupta dynasty ruled between the year 320 to 550 CE on a large part of the northern Indian subcontinent. Although the Gupta empire did not include the region of the Ajanta caves – this territory was at the time ruled by the Vakataka dynasty – the term Gupta art exceeds the political territories and is widely used to refer to the art of this period. Whenever I refer to Gupta art hence, I am considering not only Buddhist art, but also Brahmanical and Jain.

2 The two oldest versions of the story are found in the *Mahāvastu*, which is part of the Mahāsāṃghika tradition, and in the *Bhaiṣajyavastu* of the *Mūlasarvāstivādavinaya*. This latter version with only slightly changes became part of the *Divyāvadāna*. In the 5th century the poet Haribhaṭṭa included it in his *Jātakamālā*. Later, Kṣemendra edited it in his *Bodhisattvāvadānakalpalatā*, which was also the base for the Nepalese *Bhadrakalpāvadāna*. The story was also translated into several languages, followed by several later versions of the story in different parts of Asia (Straube 2006).

3 Besides Ajanta, the story is depicted in Nagarjunakonda in southern India, as well as on the Borobudur in Java (Jaini 1966, pl. I) and in the Kucha caves located on the Silk Route (Kizil 198 "Teufelshöhle") (Schlingloff 2000/2013: vol. 2, 35).

Fig. 1 Ajanta, Cave I, main chamber, left side-wall. Photograph © Ajanta Archives of the Saxon Academy of Sciences and Humanities, Research Centre "Buddhist Murals of Kucha on the Northern Silk Road"/ Andreas Stellmacher

Fig. 2 Ajanta, Cave I, main chamber, left side-wall. Drawing in SCHLINGLOFF *2000: vol. 3, pl. I, 2*

Fig. 3 Ajanta, Cave I, main chamber, left side-wall. Drawing © Ajanta Archives of the Saxon Academy of Sciences and Humanities, Research Centre "Buddhist Murals of Kucha on the Northern Silk Road"/ Monika Zin

hunter by SCHLINGLOFF is in fact a performer, probably a dancer, depicted in the context of a musical performance.

As mentioned before, the scene being analyzed here is placed on the left side wall of Ajanta Cave I, between the cave's left front corner and the first pillar on the left. The whole scene is structured in a horizontal rectangular composition visually dived into two parts. The left half, where the *nāga* king is lovingly embracing his queen, is structured in a circular composition framed by several attendants. This is a very traditional way of depicting loving couples in ancient Indian art. On the lower right of the couple, the figure dressed in blue, who is kneeling on the floor, touching the queen's foot with both hands, and turning the head to the right part of the depiction, stands as a visual connector between the couple and the figures placed on the right.

In the right half of the mural several persons are depicted in three vertical rows divided by columns: two on the left, three in the middle and at least three on the right part (**Fig. 3**). The painting is damaged at this point, so it is not possible to know whether there were more figures or objects painted. As mentioned before, the person standing in the middle was interpreted by SCHLINGLOFF as the hunter from the Sudhana story: The *nāgas* presented him various gems and dressed him according to his wishes. (SCHLINGLOFF 1973: 157). The figure in Ajanta is indeed wearing a very interesting piece of dress: A wide tunic of at least thigh-length with blue and white or yellowish horizontal stripes. His head is covered with a cloth that reaches the shoulders. Below the cloth, long cascades of locks are visible. Surrounding this figure there are at least four females playing percussion instruments. Two of them play cymbals while the other two strike sticks. The head of a fifth female is recognizable, as is part of a cylindrical object placed in front of her.[4] To show musicians surrounding a dancer is a very traditional way of depicting musical ensembles in ancient Indian art.

In the same cave, there is another musical performance depicted which is one of the most popular paintings in Ajanta (**Fig. 4**). This mural represents the virtuous king Janaka who renounced palace life to become an ascetic. As in the example described before, the royal couple is depicted surrounded by the courtiers while the musical performance is taking place (SCHLINGLOFF 2000/2013: vol. 1, 182). Both musical performance and court scene are visually connected by a diagonal axis that goes down from the royal couple to the performance. Next to the couple, there is a figure kneeling on the floor touching the queen´s feet, partially hidden by a column. As in the scene in Fig. 1, this character is also turning its head towards the musical performance and serves as a connector between the two scenes. The performance is depicted as a musical ensemble of female musicians surrounding a female dancer. That the pattern "royal couple in front of musical performance" is repeated in two different murals in Ajanta Cave I may also reinforce the idea that the scene in Fig. 1 indeed depicts a musical performance.

The performer in the scene in Fig. 3 is dressed in a striped long tunic. It had at least thigh-length but due to the deterioration of the painting it is not possible to ascertain how long the tunic was, and whether the figure wore

4 On the upper left of this composition, there is a male figure playing an instrument identified by ZIN as a *vīṇā* (ZIN 2004: 334). Although also playing music, I think this figure does not belong to the group of performers mentioned before. The same could be said about the female figure on the upper right.

Fig. 4 Ajanta, Cave I, main chamber, left side-wall. Drawing in S*CHLINGLOFF* *2000: vol. 1, 182*

trousers or not. Although they have been traditionally interpreted as elements foreign to Indian culture, tunics are not unusual in Ajanta. There are plenty of depictions that show long tunics, especially worn by horse riders (BEHL 2005: 204). These tunics nevertheless are usually tied with a belt and combined with boots and a conical cap, and none of them has the sophisticated ornamentation painted on the tunic of the dancer in Fig. 1. This textile displays stripes with different patterns painted on them (**Fig. 3**). None of them seems to be exotic. The first two rows show a pattern of concentrical circles. Similar ornaments appear among the patterns decorating the ceilings of Ajanta Cave IX, as well as within narrative depictions of the later period (ZIN 2003: vol. 1, 51–4b). The third and fifth row show a bird-like pattern. The goose motive is the most popular one among the animals' ornamental paintings. It is also depicted in Ajanta as a textile pattern (ZIN 2003: vol. 1, 92, detail 1). The fourth stripe consists of a row of undetermined designs. This could be a kind of diamond, or a flower painted with imprecision, both used to represent textile patterns (ZIN 2003: vol. 1, 53, no. 4f3 det.17). The bulls that appear in the last row also find some parallels among the ornamental paintings (ZIN 2003: vol. 1, 92, no. 8b). Unlike the tunic, the hairstyle and ornaments of the dancer correspond to the Indian Gupta style.

The performer in Ajanta Cave I is not an exceptional depiction. There are similar dancers wearing tunics depicted in Indian art. In the caves of Bagh, for example, located 300 km north of Ajanta and also dated to the 5th

Fig. 5 Bagh, Cave I. Drawing in Marshall *1927: plate D and E*

century CE, there is another well-known depiction of a musical performance. This painting was interpreted by Zin as the story of the king Māndhātar (Zin 2001). The musical scene shows two parallel performances: each group consists of a male dancer in the center surrounded by female musicians playing percussion instruments (**Fig. 5**). Most of them strike sticks and play cymbals. On the lower right of each group there is also a female musician playing a particular drum. This instrument is frequently depicted in Gupta art. It has the form of a sand-clock and is played by the drummer with the right hand, while the left hand regulates the tension of the batter head to modify the sound of the instrument. Zin believes this instrument corresponds to the *tantrīpaṭahika* mentioned in the *Harṣacarita* (Zin 2004: 340). According to Zin the two parallel performances in Bagh would express the idea of Indra's heaven being shared with (and split in two for) the king Māndhātar. For the present study the dresses of both dancers are of particular interest since they show some similarities with the one worn by the performer previously described. The one on the left is depicted in triple-bend posture, which suggests a dancing movement. His head is covered with a cloth that goes to the shoulders. He wears a thigh-long tunic with pointed ends, which unlike the one depicted in Fig. 1 is held by a waist belt. The figure also wears trousers beneath the tunic. Covering shoulders and chest is a piece of dress that was identified by Compareti as a camail originally from Central Asia (Compareti 2014). The dancer on the right is similarly dressed, only without any cloth or cap covering his head. His hand gestures resemble the ones of the Fig. 1 performer but inverting the hands. He is also standing in a balanced pose. Compareti interprets these figures as foreigners from the north, probably Bactrians (Compareti 2014: 41). As in the scene described above, the hairstyle and ornaments of the dancers correspond to Indian culture. Although the dancers depicted in Bagh wear a camail ab-

Fig. 6 Deogarh, Daśāvatāra temple. Photo: Kaufmann *1981: p. 162*

sent in the depiction reproduced in Fig. 1, the rest of the elements are strongly similar.

On the Daśāvatāra temple in Deogarh, dedicated to Viṣṇu and dated to the 6th century CE, there are three reliefs showing dancing scenes (Vats 1952: Plate XXVI (a) and (b)). Each of these panels, originally located on the temple's projection of the plinth, depicts not a male but a female dancer wearing a northern-style dress surrounded by four female musicians playing sticks, cymbals and a *tantrīpaṭahika* drum (**Fig. 6**). All three dancers are dressed in a top and a long skirt with pointed ends. Only one of the skirts depicted has a horizontal wavy pattern. The musicians are dressed in a traditional Indian Gupta fashion, i. e. long skirts with wide, ornamented girdles and bare upper body. Each of the three scenes depicts the dancer placed in the middle with two musicians on the left and two on the right side. The *tantrīpaṭahika* drum players are always standing on the right side of the scene.

Everything said about the three panels in Deogarh also matches both dancing scenes depicted in Bagh: a dancer dressed in "northern style" is surrounded by female figures dressed in a very common Indian way while playing percussion instruments. Again, the instruments are cymbals, sticks and a *tantrīpaṭahika* drum. And exactly as in the Deogarh panels, the drum player in both scenes is placed on the right.

Fig. 7 Drum player. Ajanta, Cave I, main chamber, left side-wall. Photograph © Ajanta Archives of the Saxon Academy of Sciences and Humanities, Research Centre "Buddhist Murals of Kucha on the Northern Silk Road"/ Andreas Stellmacher (line drawing by Mercedes Tortorici)

As mentioned before, in the performance depicted as part of the Sudhana story, four female musicians playing cymbals and sticks are easily recognizable. Since the right part of the scene has suffered a considerable amount of damage no more complete figures are preserved. Nevertheless, part of the head of a female figure, a bit of her pearled necklace, and the end of a brown cylindrical object can still be distinguished. Based on the pattern of composition employed in the representation of the musical performances in Bagh and Deogarh, this figure may be the drum player and the cylindrical object one end of his *tantrīpaṭahika* drum (**Fig. 7**). This supposition is further justified by the fact that the performance in Fig. 1 also follows the pattern of a dancer dressed in the "northern style" while ornamented and surrounded by figures dressed and ornamented in the Indian fashion of the time.

Conclusion

Even though an alternative identification of the dancer's scene remains open, some interesting facts can be drawn from the comparison of the musical performances mentioned above.

The musicians in every depiction are female, however the dancers can be either male or female. There seems to be no rule that determines the gender of the dancer. They all share the same type of "northern-style" dress, while the headdress and ornaments of the dancer, as well as the surrounding musicians, in all cases are depicted in an Indian Gupta style. This was probably just a dressing tradition for certain performers, maybe for a particular musical style; an idea further supported by the fact that all musicians are only playing percussion instruments: sticks, cymbals and the *tantrīpaṭahika* drum.

In Gupta times, the viewer was probably able to immediately recognize which kind of dance and music was depicted in the scenes described above. For the modern observer it will probably remain unknown whether this particular musical and dancing style had a special connotation in the ancient Indian or Buddhist context.

Although the depiction of a dancer instead of a hunter might question Schlingloff's interpretation of this particular scene, this does not imply that the identification of the entire mural has to be called into question. The scenes depicted on the left front wall correspond to the Sudhana narration, as identified by Schlingloff.

BIBLIOGRAPHY

BEHL, Benoy (2005) *The Ajanta Caves: Ancient Paintings of Buddhist India.* London.

COMPARETI, Mateo (2014) Some examples of Central Asian decorative elements in Ajanta and Bagh Indian paintings. *The Silk Road* (Saratoga) 12: 39–48.

JAINI, Padmanabh (1966) The Story of Sudhana and Manoharā: An Analysis of the Texts and the Borobudur Reliefs. *Bulletin of the School of Oriental and African Studies* (London) 29(3): 533–58.

KAUFMANN, Walter (1981) *Altindien.* Leipzig.

MARSHALL, John, ed. (1927) The Bagh Caves in the Gwalior state. London.

SCHLINGLOFF, Dieter (1973) Prince Sudhana and the Kinnarī. *Indologica Taurinensia* (Torino) 1: 155–67.

—— (2000) *Ajanta – Handbuch der Malereien 1. Erzählende Wandmalereien.* 2 vol. Wiesbaden.

—— (2013) *Ajanta – Handbook of the Paintings 1. Narrative Wall-paintings.* 2 vol. New Delhi.

STRAUBE, Martin (2006) *Prinz Sudhana und die Kinnarī: Eine buddhistische Liebesgeschichte von Kṣemendra. Texte, Übersetzung und Studie.* Marburg.

VATS, Madho Sarup (1952) *The Gupta Temple at Deogarh.* Delhi (Memoirs of the Archaeological Survey of India 70).

VATSYAYAN, Kapila (1977) *Classical Indian Dance in Literature and the Arts.* New Delhi.

—— (1982) *Dance in Indian Painting.* New Delhi.

ZIN, Monika (2001) The Identification of the Bagh Painting. *East and West* (Rome) 51/3–4: 299–322.

—— (2003). *Ajanta: Handbuch Der Malereien = Handbook of the Paintings 2: Devotionale und ornamentale Malereien. 2 vol.* Wiesbaden.

—— (2004) Die altindischen vīṇās. *Musikarchäologie IV. Musikarchäologische Quellengruppen: Bodenurkunden, mündliche Überlieferung,* ed. E. Hickmann & R. Eichmann, Rahden: 321–62 (= Orient-Archäologie 15).

Deutsche Zusammenfassung

Auf einer Wandmalerei in Ajanta Höhle I, die Schlingloff als Darstellung der Sudhana-Geschichte interpretierte, zeigt eine Szene eine männliche Figur, die mit einer eigentümlichen langen, gestreiften Tunika bekleidet ist. Schlingloff identifizierte diese Figur als einen Jäger, der in der Mūlasarvāstivāda-Version der Geschichte erwähnt wird. Ich lege hier dar, warum es sich bei der dargestellten Figur nicht um einen Jäger, sondern eher um einen männlichen Tänzer handelt. Die Szene weist starke Ähnlichkeiten mit musikalischen Darbietungen auf, die in Bagh und Deogarh dargestellt sind.

The Great Blue –
Tiles from Punjab on Display in the Museum für Asiatische Kunst at the Humboldt Forum, Berlin.

Dorina Michaelis

The name, the Great Blue, caught my eye as I was examining online photographs from the Lyallpur Museum in Faisalabad, Pakistan. One of the displays, in their small exhibition space, is filled with blue and white tiles from different locations in the region. It is presented next to other exhibits that show the great cultural achievements of the region from the times of the Indus civilisation up to the modern day. "How wonderful", I thought, "that the people value these tiles the same way as they do with objects of presumably greater significance and see them as equals in their own display at a prominent location."

In Islamic art and architecture, tilework plays an important part of research. European museums are filled with tiles from different regions and times throughout the Islamic world. Numerous books have been published on different aspects and various researchers have built their whole career on the subject. However, the tilework from South Asia seems to have always been looked at with less regard. To this day there has not been a complete study about tilework from South Asia.

This article will give a brief overview of important tiled buildings in Multan (Pakistan), introduce the craft of tile production and take a closer look at some of the tiles on display in the Museum für Asiatische Kunst at the Humboldt Forum.

Punjab and the history of tilework

Tilework in South Asia is certainly limited to a small number of regions, with a large quantity of objects coming from Sindh and the Pakistani part of the Punjab. Tilework can be found in other regions as well, but to a much smaller degree. Explanations for this are inconclusive. Building traditions and the local climate, being beneficial for the survival of brick architecture, certainly had a significant influence. Migration patterns of artisans and closer connections to craftspeople in the adjacent regions in Afghanistan and Iran might have also played an important role in the development of the craft.

Although most of the tiles on display at the Humboldt Forum are from Sindh, this article will focus on the ones from Punjab.

The Punjab, literally the land of five rivers (from Persian *panǧ* five and *āb* water), is located in the North-West of the subcontinent and stretches across the five rivers Indus, Jhelum, Chenab, Ravi and Sutlej. Frembgen includes in his description of the Punjab the river Beas that is located east of the Sutlej but excludes the Indus (2003: 133). Singh states that after the partition of Pakistan and India, the Indian Punjab remained the land of five rivers, being the Ravi, Beas, Sutlej, Sarasvati and Yamuna (Singh 1989: 1). This shows how diverse the term is defined and used.

The historical Punjab varied in size, from the area between the Indus and the Sutlej during the Mughal period to being bordered to the west by the Sulaiman Mountain range and extending to the east as far as Delhi under British rule (Grewal 1998: 1). Today it is divided by the Pakistani Indian border. Major cities of historic significance are Lahore and Multan, with Rawalpindi and Bahawalpur increasing in importance under British rule. Unlike Sindh (predominately controlled independently by local rulers), the Punjab was often part of the larger domain of the northern Indian empires. The Punjab is often associated with Sufism (*ṣūfīya)* and Islamic spirituality but even more so with the emergence of Sikhism.

While Lahore was the imperial centre, Multan remained the regional capital and home to *ṣūfī* saints of various orders. Its name is so closely connected to tile-

Fig. 1 Tomb of Yūsuf Gardīzī in Multan. © Wikipedia/Junaidahmadj. 2011

work that blue and white tiles from Pakistan are often referred to as "Multan tiles", sometimes with the addition of "from Sindh" which contradicts the definition as "Multan tiles". This adds to the already existing difficulties in correctly identifying and attributing tiles to a specific location.

The origins of tilework for both regions remain somewhat obscure. The lack of reliable data on building dates and various renovations of buildings over the past centuries makes it difficult to name an exact moment when tiles became an architectural feature.

For the Punjab, the introduction of tilework points to the 14th and 15th century which coincides with the reign of the Timurids whose architecture and tilework in Central Asia shows a remarkable resemblance. A notable building for its tilework is the mausoleum of Shah Rukn-i 'Ālam (1251–1335) in Multan. According to KHAN the construction date remains unclear as there is no contemporary source to consult[1] (KHAN 1983: 218f.). Others state that it was built by Ghiyath al-Din Tughluq between 1320 and 1324, when he was the sultan of Delhi (DEGEORGE & PORTER 2002: 244).[2] Although it bears less tiles than other buildings, it is often referred to for its tilework and quoted as the role model for funereal architecture in the region.[3]

Other notable mausoleums in Multan for their tilework are the tombs of Bahā-ud-Din Zakariya (1171–1262), Shams Sabzwari (1165–1276), Sultan 'Alī Akbar and the tomb of Yūsuf Gardīzī. All of them underwent heavy re-construction over time so none can be considered reliable sources for the historical development of tiles.

Zakariya's tomb was rebuilt after it was destroyed in the siege of Multan in 1848 (CUNNINGHAM 1875: 131). Several tiles were still in situ, bearing inscriptions of repairs and restorations, especially those from 1902 (KHAN 1983: 192).

The mausoleum of Shams Sabzwari is recognisable for its tiled dome in bright green colour. CUNNINGHAM states that it was "surmounted by a hemispherical dome covered with glazed sky-blue tiles" when he visited Multan[4] (CUNNINGHAM 1875: 134). Originally built in 1329, it seems to be entirely re-built in 1779 (KHAN 1983: 206).

Sultan 'Alī Akbar's tomb is often referred to as "the little Rukn-i 'Alam" (KHAN 1983: 236). The exterior exhibits the known style of tilework in horizontal panels but is more decorated than its big brother.

Yūsuf Gardīzī's tomb (**Fig. 1**)[5] is covered in tiles but varies heavily in architecture as it is a flat roofed building with rectangular floor plan. According to FURNIVAL,

---

1 KHAN states that Ibn Battuta (1304–1369) did not mention the building that with its height of 35 m is hard to miss (KHAN 1983: 216).

2 This leads to confusion if the official date of death for Shah Rukn-i 'Ālam is 1335. DEGEORGE and PORTER mention it was built in memory of the saint but do not state a date of death in their publication.

3 According to KHAN the mausoleum at Dera Pin Panah is a copy of the Rukn-i 'Ālam's tomb. The mausoleum of Din Panah was finished in 1602/1603 so the mausoleum of Rukn-i 'Ālam must have been built before that date.

4 CUNNINGHAM visited Multan in 1853 and recorded his observations. It is unclear if he visited again at a later date.

5 Junaidahmadj, CC BY-SA 3.0, https://creativecommons.org/licenses/by-sa/3.0/deed.en, via Wikimedia Commons, https://upload.wikimedia.org/wikipedia/commons/archive/c/

Fig. 2 Ruins of the tombs in Uch Sharif. © Wikipedia/Shah zaman baloch, 2012

it was constructed in the 1750s (1904: 123). Other flat roof tombs in Uch are dated earlier than their octagonal counterparts, which can also be assumed for the tomb of Yūsuf Gardīzī.[6] The construction FURNIVAL is referring to might have been a restoration.[7]

For the city of Uch Sharif, located about 120 km south of Multan, the most known buildings are the tombs of Ustād Nuriya, Bībī Jiwandi and Bahā'al Ḥalīm, constructed in the same architectural style as the ones in Multan with an octagonal floorplan (**Fig. 2**)[8].

Besides tombs there are other buildings, like mosques, covered in tiles. But unlike the mausoleums these are often less prominent and, due to being still used as places of worship, more difficult to access and study.

c2/20170316074253%21Tomb_of_Shah_Yousuf_Gardezi_Wallpaper.jpg.

6 KHAN divides the funeral building in Uch into two categories without giving exact dates, the earlier flat roofed building and the later with octagonal floor plan.

7 DEGEORGE and PORTER suggest that the tomb was built soon after Gardīzī's death in 1152 but tilework might have been very recent (DEGEORGE & PORTER 2002: 244).

8 Shah zaman baloch, CC BY-SA 3.0, https://creativecommons.org/licenses/by-sa/3.0/deed.en, via Wikimedia Commons, https://upload.wikimedia.org/wikipedia/commons/1/17/Tomb_of_Bibi_Jawindi.jpg.

Production of glazed ceramics in the Punjab

There are various accounts dealing with the production of ceramics from the 19th century. British officers recorded and published their observations of the local manufacture of different products including ceramics.

The most often quoted publication is GEORGE BIRDWOOD's *The Industrial Arts of India,* published in 1884. He seems to have taken his description entirely from B.H. BADEN POWELL's *Hand-Book of the Manufactures and Arts of the Punjab,* published in 1872.[9] And yet BADEN POWELL's descriptions are taken from a pamphlet published at the Central Jail in Lahore (BADEN POWELL 1872: 220). According to him ceramics were produced in several jails in Punjab, the craft originally introduced by a local.

The third account is 20 years older than BADEN POWELL's, published by C.J. HALLIFAX in 1892. HALLIFAX investigated the pottery and glass industry of the Punjab, with a focus on the production of unglazed wares for the pottery section. His intention seems to have been to give an overview of the current state of production including details like the numbers of workers and cost of materials.

9 BIRDWOOD's descriptions appear to be a summary of BADEN POWELL's remarks. It is also possible that BIRDWOOD took the description directly from the Lahore Central jail pamphlet.

These accounts mostly deal with the production of domestic ware and less with tiles as these were not of interest as export products for the British home market.

Although the basics of production between tiles and domestic wares do not differ significantly, the details of the ceramic making process will be taken from the survey conducted by a research team in 1971, associated with the Smithsonian Institute in Washington, D.C. and the University of New South Wales in Sydney (RYE 1976: xiii). In Multan the researchers interviewed and observed the work of a local potter master whose workshop was one of five existing in the city and was operated by the Pakistan Government's Small Industries Corporation (RYE 1976: 89).

The clay (*miṭṭī*) was prepared by adding sand in a ratio of 4:1 and dried in the sun depending on the clay's initial degree of moisture (RYE 1976: 90). According to the potter interviewed all potters in Multan used the same clay deposit that to his understanding has been used for more than 200 years and was located outside the city (RYE 1976: 90). In Punjab, and also in Sindh, the clay is of brick red colour after firing. In other adjacent Islamic regions, the material of choice for tiles is "frit ware", a mixture of clay, pounded quartz and frit, a combination of glass and sodium carbonite (DEGEORGE & PORTER 2002: 13).[10] Frit ware is usually grey in colour and a very hard material. The red burning brick clay used in Punjab and Sindh easily disintegrates what may as well be the reason for the need of restoration in short intervals.

Tiles were formed by hand, roughly shaped and later trimmed to size, taking into account the shrinkage due to drying and firing (RYE 1976: 93). In bone-dry conditions they were prepared for slipping, decoration and glazing (RYE 1976: 93).

The two basic ingredients used for the glaze were quarzite stone (*karunḍ*) and calcined plant ash (*khār*). Borax was usually added and glass in cullet form might have been added by some potters (RYE 1976: 94). *karunḍ* and *khār* were ground into powder and later mixed. Water was added to the mixture to moisten it enough to form it into a ball (RYE 1976: 95). A similar process is described by BADEN POWELL, mixing the ingredients with water and forming a ball the size of an orange (1892: 221).

The ball was put into a kiln at the end of a firing process for sintering and left until the kiln cooled down after three to four days (RYE 1976: 95). The ball was then crushed into a powder to which borax or ground glass was added (RYE 1976: 96). The addition of ordinary glass instead of borax was reasonable considering the economic situation. The interviewed potter mentioned that the use of ordinary cullet, bottle and window glass by other potters as cheap replacement for other materials results in an inferior quality of the glaze, the flaking-off of glaze more readily and increased crazing (RYE 1976: 96). This is important to note because observations of a larger number of tiles have shown that there is indeed a difference between glaze qualities, by colour and surface as well as the amount of crazing and flaking.

The mixture of *karunḍ, khār* and borax was filled into a crucible and placed in the kiln for firing. The materials fused once again and the finished product was ground into fine powder after cooling. This powder, used as the final glaze, is called *kac* (RYE 1976: 96), a term that is familiar from the earlier written accounts. BADEN POWELL mentions a material called "kánch" (1872: 220). According to him, there is *angrezi kānchi* and *desī kānchi,* translated by BIRDWOOD into "English glaze" and "country glaze" (BIRDWOOD 1884: 307).

The white siliceous slip used in Multan was made of *kac* and *karunḍ*, mixed in a ratio of 1:1 (RYE 1976: 96f.). The slip did not contain any white clay, like kaolin, as would be expected.

Both the glaze and slip powder were sieved and water was gradually added to reach the required degree of liquidity (RYE 1976: 98). A liquid glue made by boiling wheat flour in water was added which matches the description of BADEN POWELL that glaze is mixed with "'māwā,' a glutinous substance made with 'nishāsta,' the gluten obtained by washing wheat flower and collecting the subsidence" (BADEN POWELL 1892: 225).

For the decoration, the traditional colour palette of blue (*lājvard*), turquoise (*sabzī*) and white (*cittā*) was expanded by a light blue, similar to turquoise, according to RYE and EVANS. They also mentioned that since the 1960s some Multan potters have expanded their colour palette further by using green, brown and yellow (RYE 1976: 98). BADEN POWELL already mentions the use of other colours, like yellow and different shades of green (BADEN POW-

10 In 1300 Abu'l-Qasim bin Ali bin Muhammad bin Abu Tahir, a historian at the Mongol court and member of the leading ceramic family from Kashan, the center of pottery production in Iran, wrote a treatise about the production of ceramics that has been used as the most prominent resource for researchers.

ELL 1892: 223f.). Blue was based on cobalt oxide and mixed with black copper oxide in a ratio of 4:1. For turquoise only black copper oxide was used (RYE 1976: 99).

The chosen motif was either applied by hand with a graphite pencil or a paper template was used by piercing holes into it and after putting it in place dusting it with charcoal (RYE 1976: 99). For tiles, each tilemaker had a number of designs customers could choose from or, if necessary, designs could be adjusted to customer's needs (RYE 1976: 93). The chosen designs were applied and filled with colour and when dried, covered in glaze. Finally, the tiles and other objects were placed in the kiln and fired.

One detail that shall not go unnoticed is the type of potter's wheel used in Pakistan. According to RYE and EVANS the dominate wheel was the so-called pit wheel or kick wheel where the wheel is placed in a pit as the name suggest and kicked into movement with the feet. This wheel or variations thereof was used in other Islamic countries, e.g. Afghanistan. In India the wheel most commonly used was the single wheel or true potter's wheel that is placed on the ground and put in motion by hand (RYE 1976: 116). HALLIFAX mentioned the existence of two types of potter's wheel, one that is placed on the ground and one that is placed in a hole (HALLIFAX 1892: 4).

The differences of potter's wheels in India and Pakistan may suggest that at some point potters from other regions migrated to what is now Pakistan and introduced their method of production. The use of the single wheel was limited to a few places in Sindh, as Hala and Karachi. The introduction of the pit wheel apparently dates to the beginning of the 20th century (RYE 1976: 116). If this is the case, it might be an additional indication that the introduction of the production of glazed ceramics to Sindh came from a different place as it did for the Punjab.

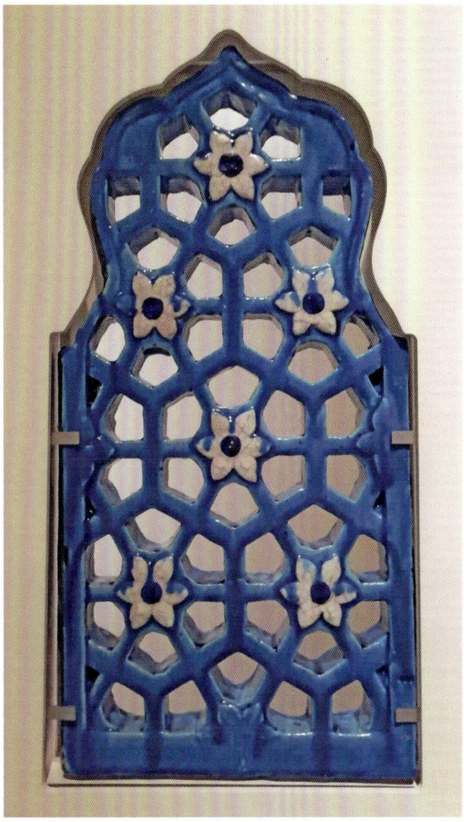

Fig. 3 Acc. No. I 2839, 18th–19th century, earthenware, underglaze painting. Museum für Asiatische Kunst, SMB © Dorina Michaelis, 2022

Decoration and motif

In terms of decor and motif, there are two main subjects that appear individually and combined: geometric and floral patterns. Although the exact dating of tiles largely remains an issue, it can be noticed that there is a shift over time from a preference of geometric patterns to floral motifs. While buildings from the 15th and 16th century are mostly covered in tiles with geometric patterns, later buildings from the 18th and especially 19th century are predominantly decorated with floral motifs.[11]

The geometric patterns are closely connected to Islamic traditions that prefer non-figurative motifs. In line with the art and architecture of other countries with a predominantly Muslim population, different shapes in alternating colours follow a strict geometric principle. The tiles on display in the Museum für Asiatische Kunst are from later periods, so there are more floral motifs or a combination of floral and geometric patterns.[12] But even the tiles with dominant floral decorations show the underlying principles of geometry, into which the highly stylized depictions of plants are fitted. Three examples of geometric pattern from Punjab are the *jālī*, Acc. No. I 2839, I 2840 and I 2850 (**Fig. 3, 4**). *Jālī*, from Sanskrit *jāla* meaning net, is a latticed or perforated screen and is a popular feature in South Asian architecture. Its style varies from simple cross patterns to elaborate designs like the ones on the west wall of the Sidi Saiyyed Mosque in Ahmedabad, Gujarat.

The *jālī*, I 2839 and I 2840 (**Fig. 3**), are identical in shape, angular on the bottom with a curved arch at the top. The main geometrical motif is a hexagon, divided on its sides by lines that lead to a six petalled flower in the

11 Exact statements about the decoration of buildings remain vague as it is often unknown when and in what way buildings were renovated in the past.

12 Tile I 2794 from Sindh is the only tile without any floral ornaments.

middle. The colour palette is typical for the Punjab, with white and dark blue for the flowers and a vibrant turquoise throughout.

The third one, I 2850 (**Fig. 4**), is a square tile with a small middle section cut out. The eight petalled flower in the middle is surrounded by a hexagon, divided by lines that create cut-out spaces in the form of bow-ties and uneven shaped pentagons. The hexagon itself is bordered by a small square frame of cut outs in the form of eight pointed stars. It is glazed in the same colours as I 2839 and I 2840, with a white and dark blue flower and turquoise but in a lighter shade.

Fig. 4 Acc. No. I 2850, 18th–19th century, earthenware, underglaze painting. Museum für Asiatische Kunst, SMB © Dorina Michaelis, 2022

These tiles are not entirely covered in glaze on their back side. This suggests that the placement at their original location was out of sight of the visitor. While often used as dividers to separate a public from a private space in Mughal architecture, smaller *jālī* like the ones on display were used to provide a light source in the upper levels of a building or inside of a dome.

A further study of the variety of geometrical designs used in the region would be necessary to determine the stylistic similarities and differences in other parts of the Islamic world.

Examples for the use of floral designs in the later phase are the tiles I 2841 to I 2844 (**Fig. 5**). Of this set of four tiles, two each are nearly identical in design. On I 2843 and I 2844 (the outer two) there are living plants with six and nine different flowers. The plant is accompanied by a smaller plant on each side with four and six leaves and a flower bud. The scene is framed by a curved arch in the familiar style of Mughal architecture, ornamented with flowers and buds. I 2842 and I 2841 are also framed by a curved arch, and on each side there is a half column with capital and base in the floral shape.[13] When placed directly next to each other, an arcade is created that might point to the airy nature of imperial garden architecture.

The flowers are placed in a vase on an elevated plate, accompanied by grapes on each side and in the case of I 2842 pomegranates were added. Flowers in vases and flowers in general, framed in niches or arches are a popular subject, especially in Mughal architecture and art. The most outstanding example from the region being the Wazir Khan Mosques, built between 1634 and 1641 in Lahore (**Fig. 6**)[14].

The identification of individual flowers is often complex as it seems they are generic and taken from existing templates or simply products of the artist's imagination. For tiles, it is particularly difficult as the medium is prone to blurring clear lines and blending colours in the firing process. In this case, however, the flowers are clearly drawn and to some degree identifiable.

For I 2842, the flower in the middle of the arrangement might be identified as a rose or marigold and the one above it as a violet. The remaining four, two on each side and paired opposite each other, are more difficult to distinguish. They might be a local variety of daffodils.

The flower in the centre on I 2841 seems to be a chrysanthemum or dahlia, surrounded by pairs of lilies and irises. The one above the centre might again be a daffodil variant or with its stamens a lily or hibiscus. Important to note is that the tripartite calyx is shaped like the flower bud on the arch above and is a recurring element in the decoration of tiles from Punjab.

I 2843 and I 2844 are decorated with lilies, irises, carnations, violets and again possible variations of daf-

13 This feature can be found on larger ceramic architectural elements, e.g. the tiled dome from Pakistan at the Hetjens Museum in Düsseldorf.

14 Noor Soban, CC BY-SA 4.0, https://creativecommons.org/licenses/by-sa/4.0/deed.en, via Wikimedia Commons, https://upload.wikimedia.org/wikipedia/commons/8/8b/Wazir_Khan_Mosque_DSC_0778.jpg, cropped.

Fig. 5 Acc. No. I 2843, I 2842, I 2841, I 2844 (from left to right), 18th–19th century, earthenware, underglaze painting. Museum für Asiatische Kunst, SMB © Dorina Michaelis, 2022

fodils. The flower in the centre of the arrangement of I 2844 might be a local variant of jasmine.

Flowers and plants play an important part in Islamic art as they are a reminder of the paradise garden mentioned in the *Qur'ān*. They are an omnipresent element not only in architectural decoration but also in textile and metal art, other decorative arts and painting. They also are almost omnipresent in poetry and *ṣūfī* literature, so it comes as no surprise to find them in connection with *ṣūfī* funeral architecture.

Similar flowers as mentioned above can also be found on the disc-shaped tile I 2849 (**Fig. 8**). Together with I 2848 (**Fig. 7**), these two are the strangest tiles on display. One reason is the unusual shape, the other reason is the fact that they are decorated on both sides of the disc. Tiles are only glazed and decorated on one side for obvious reason. One can only speculate for what these discs were used. Possible is a usage simply as an object of decoration for European consumers, as a souvenir from exotic and foreign lands. It might also have been used as a sample piece for the different styles of decoration a costumer could choose from at a workshop. The same might apply to the three square tiles I 2845 to I 2847 that are also decorated and glazed on both sides.

Fig. 6 Mosaik tile panels on the exterior of the Wazir Khan Mosque (built 1634–1641). © Wikipedia/Noor Soban, 2017

Both tiles are circular in shape and about 1.3 cm thick. Both discs have a dark and a light side, one side where the motif is applied on a white background and

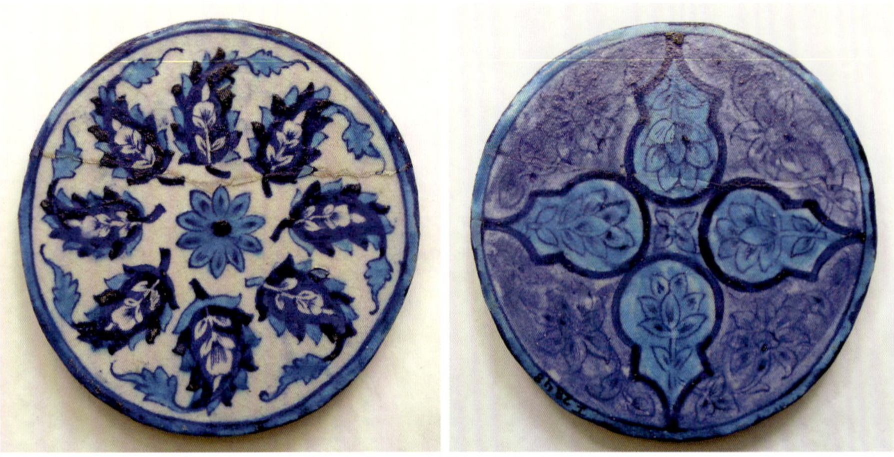

Fig. 7 Acc. No. I 2848, 18th–19th century, earthenware, underglaze painting. Museum für Asiatische Kunst, SMB © Dorina Michaelis, 2014

one side with a blue background. The rim on the light side is painted in dark blue, framing the inner motif. In each case the motif is arranged circularly around a central flower.

I 2848's central flower has ten petals in turquoise with inner and outer lining in dark blue. It is surrounded by eight leaves in tear-drop shape with a curved upper end. This motif is called as *boteh* or *buta* but more commonly known in Europe as paisley. The inside of each *buta* is decorated with a small flower in white on dark blue background. On the sides, there are leaves in dark blue and turquoise. A small leaf is added to the upper end of each *buta*.

The other side of I 2848 has a blue background surrounded by a small turquoise frame. The main motif consists of four opposing shapes, circular in the middle of the disc and pointed towards the edge. Each is outlined in dark blue and shows a flower with seven petals and two small leaves on the side on a turquoise background. The spaces in between are filled with a flower and leaves. In the middle of the disc is a small four petalled flower.

I 2849 (**Fig. 8**) is decorated in similar fashion, with the eight petalled central flower in dark blue, a smaller white one of six petals in the middle and eight small leaves in turquoise surrounding them. Two interlooping tendrils with flowers, flower buds and leaves are secluding the scene. The flower is the same one as mentioned above on the dark side of I 2848 and together with the tripartite bud a recurring motif on Multan ceramics. Unusual is the long thin leaf that resembles the *saz* leaf, a popular motif on the ceramics of the Ottoman empire.

The other side is similar to the previous one with a small turquoise frame on the rim and an overall blue ground. The motif is closer to the ones on the light side with central eight petalled flower and leaves and tendril with leaves surrounding it. With the tendril's curled sections and the shape of the leaves, it appears to be a vine branch. Although generally looked down upon among Muslims, the consumption of wine is a common subject in poetry and *ṣūfī* literature, associated with their search for a closer connection to God.

Inscriptions are the third element of decorations and can be found as an individual form of exterior decoration. Often, they are displayed in panels above doors or framing them or larger bands on the upper part of interior walls. Depending on the nature of the building, being a mosque or a mausoleum, the length of the inscription varies. Larger sections of the *Qur'ān* or other religious literature might be quoted. Smaller sections often con-

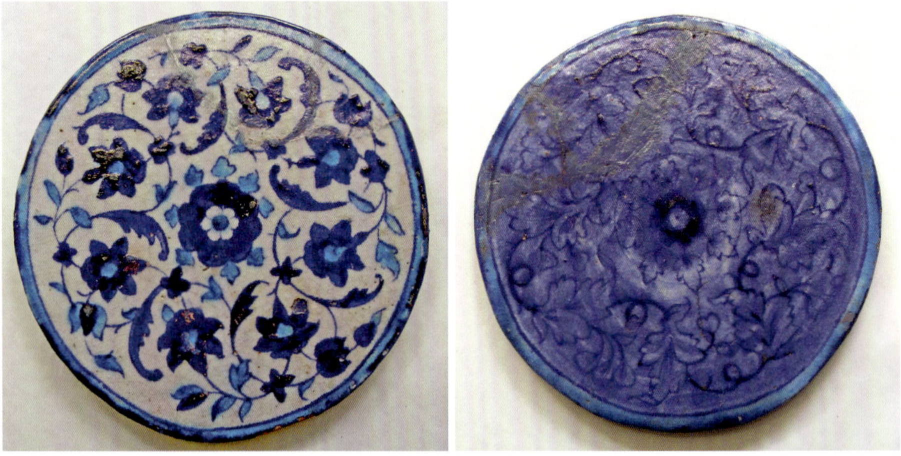

Fig. 8 Acc. No. I 2849, 18th–19th century, earthenware, underglaze painting. Museum für Asiatische Kunst, SMB © Dorina Michaelis, 2014

Fig. 9 Acc. No. I 2837, 18th–19th century, earthenware, underglaze painting. Museum für Asiatische Kunst, SMB © Dorina Michaelis, 2022

sist of blessings or prayers that are used in everyday life. The tile I 2837 (**Fig. 9**) shows such a prayer. Compared to other inscription tiles, it is a small panel of four tiles. The middle section bears the inscription in white on dark blue background. This section is framed by two smaller horizontal bands decorated each with a tendril with flower bud and leaves in turquoise and dark blue on a white background. As the inscription is not framed by borders of tendril and flower buds on its left and right side, it might be possible that it was originally part of a larger inscription. It is unusual however that there is empty space at the beginning and end of the inscription as inscriptions in Arabic are mostly arranged close together in an artistic manner.

Jürgen Frembgen who studied the contemporary practices of Muslims in Pakistan intensely describes the use of Arabic script as decoration on buildings, such as tombs, as "Manifestation islamischer Spiritualität" (a manifestation of Islamic spirituality) (2010: 225). He also states that often inscriptions tell less about the religious affiliations, being part of the *sunni* or *shī'a* lineage, and more about the religious identity of parishioners and the social environment of the deceased (Frembgen 2010: 225). If this also applies to the religious practices of the past remains inconclusive.

One architectural feature that needs to be mentioned but is barely present in museums is the glazed brick and, as a more sophisticated form, the moulded glazed brick. As one of the oldest forms of glazed decorations on buildings, it can be seen as the original starting point for tilework and is, in this context, to be associated with the Timurid architecture of Central Asia and Iran. It can be found on buildings associated to the late 15th century like the tomb of Bībī Jiwandi in Uch and the tomb of Ghazi Khan in Dera Ghazi Khan.

Dating of tiles

The dating of tiles from Punjab and Sindh has proven to be a difficult task for various reasons. While the basis for dating ceramics in other regions is provided by excavations and systematic documentation, little record is accessible concerning tiles from South Asia. Many tiles found in European collections have a somewhat obscure biography, meaning they are of unknown origin. Individuals traveling to, and through, South Asia in the past centuries have picked them up at locations and years later handed them over to museums, giving vague information about their original place of origin.[15] Some may have been purchased in larger cities or at auctions in Europe.

Another aspect that makes this task even harder is the continuing restoration of monuments. From written evidence[16] we know that the British conducted large restoration measures after 1858 when they gained control of the Punjab. Monuments were evaluated and restorations took place if deemed necessary. This continued to date, with the latest on a larger scale being the restora-

15 The presented tiles at the exhibition in the Humboldt Forum were mostly acquired from Fedor Jagor in 1876.

16 Henry Hardy Cole has published several reports with the title "Preservation of National Monuments" in the 1880s in his capacity as Curator of Ancient Monuments.

tion of the tombs of the Talpur Mirs in Hyderabad, Sindh in 2015/16.

Closely connected to restoration measures is the continuation of traditional designs and motifs.

Closing remarks

Like with the other Great Blues in our world, the ocean and the sky, the more we have learned, the more we have realised how little we know and how much there is still to explore. The same applies to the tilework of Punjab and Sindh as well as to ceramic production of South Asia in general. Although tiles are on display in many museums, their origins have not yet been studied beyond their general connection to architectural monuments. Material analysis have only been conducted in a few cases and can tell us only so much without further information. Until additional research is conducted and published, statements concerning origins and age of tiles and even the history of tilework remain inconclusive.

Bibliography

Baden Powell, B.H. (1872) *Hand-Book of the Manufactures and Arts of the Punjab, with a combined glossary and index of vernacular trades and technical terms, forming vol. II to the "Hand-Book of the Economic Products of the Punjab"*. Lahore.

Birdwood, George C.M. (1884) *The Industrial Arts of India*. London.

Cunningham, Alexander (1875) *Report for the year 1872–73*. Calcutta (Archaeological Survey of India Vol. V).

DeGeorge, Gérard & Porter, Yves (2002) *The Art of the Islamic Tile*. Paris.

Frembgen, Jürgen Wasim (2003) *Nahrung für die Seele*. München.

Frembgen, Jürgen Wasim (2010) Kalligraphie in der Welt pakistanischer Sufi-Schreine. *Die Aura des Alif, Schriftkunst im Islam*, Ed. J.W. Frembgen. München.

Furnival, William James (1904) *Leadless decorative tiles, faience and mosaic: comprising notes and excerpts on the history, materials, manufacture & use of ornamental flooring tiles, ceramic mosaic, and decorative tiles and faience with complete series of recipes for tile-bodies and for leadless glazes and art-tile enamels*. Staffordshire.

Grewal, J.S. (1998) *The Sikhs of the Punjab*. The New Cambridge History of India. Revised Edition. Cambridge.

Hallifax, C.J. (1892) *Monograph on the Pottery and Glass Production of the Punjab 1890–91*. Lahore.

Khan, Ahmad Nabi (1980) *Uchch: History and Architecture*. Islamabad. (1983) *Multan: History and Architecture*. Islamabad.

Rye, Owen S. & Evans, Clifford (1976) *Traditional Pottery Techniques of Pakistan: field and laboratory studies*. Washington (Smithsonian contributions to anthropology, no.21).

Singh, Ganda (1989) *History and Culture of Panjab through the Ages. History and Culture of Panjab*. Ed. Mohinder Singh. New Delhi.

Deutsche Zusammenfassung

Zwar nicht zum ersten Mal, aber erstmals in größerer Zahl sind kunstvoll bemalte Fliesen aus Pakistan Teil der neuen Dauerausstellung im Museum für Asiatische Kunst Berlin. Keramik aus Südasien gehört zu den eher vernachlässigten und allgemein unbekannten Themen der Forschung. Der vorliegende Artikel betrachtet einige der im Humboldt Forum ausgestellten Fliesen aus dem Punjab näher. Neben einer Einführung in den Forschungsstand und in die Architektur Multans wird auf die Herstellung von Keramik in der Region, deren Verwendung und Symbolik der Dekorelemente eingegangen.

Die Umāmaheśvara-Stele von Chatrarhi: Das 3D-Modell als Studienobjekt

Gerald Kozicz

Die COVID-19-Pandemie hat seit Beginn vor zwei Jahren eine Entwicklung offensichtlich gemacht und verschärft, die sich bereits davor abgezeichnet hat und sich vor allem auch in Fachzeitschriften leicht nachvollziehen lässt: die Verschiebung der wissenschaftlichen Forschung von Themen aus der Feldforschung hin zu musealen Sammlungen. Dass die Pandemie letztendlich die Feldforschung in Asien für westliche Forschende weitgehend unmöglich gemacht hat, war nur ein weiterer, wenngleich unvorhersehbarer Impuls dahingehend, sich verstärkt den Objekten in öffentlichen wie auch privaten Sammlungen zuzuwenden. Aber bereits davor haben Museen bewusst neue Medien genutzt, um ihre Sammlungen zu digitalisieren und so in einer davor noch nie dagewesenen Qualität online zu präsentieren. Digitalisierung kann in einem Museumsbetrieb unter idealen, quasi Laborbedingungen stattfinden, und die Resultate sind dementsprechend. Ganz anders dazu ist die Situation bei der Feldforschung. In den Himalaya-Regionen ist vor allem die Tatsache erschwerend, dass viele der zu dokumentierenden Objekte oder Gebäude noch aktiv verehrt und genutzt werden und somit der Zugang nur beschränkt möglich oder zeitlich limitiert ist. Rahmenbedingungen wie Einsehbarkeit und Lichtverhältnisse sind meist bestenfalls mäßig, das Verwenden von Blitzlicht und Stativ oftmals verboten, und die Aufmerksamkeit, die man als „Fremder" bekommt, ist selten hilfreich für ein konzentriertes Arbeiten. Dass unter diesen Umständen Dokumentationen fast immer unvollständig bleiben und es oft auch keine Möglichkeit einer Wiederholung gibt, hat zur Folge, dass Datensätze für die Weiterbearbeitung oft lückenhaft bleiben. Offensichtlich wird dies meist vor allem in der Bilddokumentation, die zwar die atmosphärischen Aspekte einer religiösen Stätte und ihrer Bildkunst gut einfangen kann, aber in Bezug auf Schärfe und Vollständigkeit, wie sie für ikonographische und kunsthistorische Studien erforderlich ist, mit den Aufnahmen von Museumsobjekten fast nie mithalten kann.

Abb. 1 Nebentempel des Śaktidevī-Tempelkomplexes, Chatrarhi, Himachal Pradesh

Dass neue und sich ständig weiterentwickelnde Methoden der digitalen Dokumentation und vor allem der digitalen Darstellung auch im Kontext der Feldforschung erfolgreich eingesetzt werden können, davon handelt dieser Beitrag. Im Konkreten geht es um eine Stele, die Umāmaheśvara, also Śiva (Śaṅkara) und Pārvatī (Gaurī) im Zentrum einer komplexen Rahmenkonstruktion zeigt. Die Stele befindet sich in einem Nebentempel des

Śaktidevī-Heiligtums von Chatrarhi (auch Chatrari, Chhatrari, Chhattrarhi, Chhattrardi oder Chhatradi) in Himachal Pradesh (**Abb. 1**).[1] Publiziert wurde sie bereits von POSTEL, NEVEN und MANKODI in *Antiquities of Himachal* (1985: 73, Fig. 97), wobei neben der Abbildung in der textlichen Beschreibung nur das Paar im Zentrum erwähnt wurde. Der komplexe Gesamtaufbau, in dem die beiden Hauptgottheiten nicht einmal die Hälfte einnehmen, blieb vollkommen unbeachtet. Die etwa ins 10. Jahrhundert datierbare Skulptur fand auch Eingang in DONALDSONS zweibändiges Werk zu Śiva und Pārvatī (2007, Vol. 1 Text: 325, 327; Vol. 2 Plates: xxx, 66, Abb. C-95), wobei DONALDSON auf das oben erwähnte Bild zurückgriff und daraus nur eine Vergrößerung des zentralen Bereichs mit den beiden Hauptgottheiten abbildete.

Abb. 2 Die Umāmaheśvara-Stele

Die Stele befindet sich in einem kleinem Raum mit einer Grundfläche von etwa 6m^2 und einer Raumhöhe von ca. 2m. Einzige Lichtquelle ist die Eingangsöffnung, der gegenüber die Stele auf einem Steinsockel platziert ist. Stele und Sockel bildeten ursprünglich keine Einheit. Śiva und Pārvatī sind heute teilweise verhüllt (**Abb. 2**). Das Betreten des Raums wurde mir 2016 kurz gestattet, 2019 nicht. Allerdings durfte ich die Kamera in den Raum halten und auch das Stativ in den Raum stellen, soweit der Arm von der Schwelle aus reichte. Eine exakte Auswahl der Bildausschnitte war daher kaum möglich. Dies ergab eine Bildserie, mit der ich fast alle Bereiche der Stele mehrfach ablichten konnte. Bildserien bilden heute die Grundlage von Photogrammetrie-basierten 3D-Modellen. Es ist ein etablierter Workflow, für den aber gewisse Qualitätskriterien gelten wie etwa konstante Brennweite und eine nicht wechselnde Beleuchtungssituation. Die Erwartungen in Bezug auf die Umāmaheśvara-Stele waren aufgrund der Umstände gering, das Ergebnis umso überraschender.

Das 3D-Modell zeigt die Stele mit einer Schärfe und einer Plastizität, wie sie im Kultraum selbst nicht wahrnehmbar ist (**Abb. 3 und 4**). Während die Hauptfiguren natürlich verhüllt und mit Blumen geschmückt erscheinen – und damit aber auch die rituelle Funktion und atmosphärischen Qualitäten des Kultobjekts widerspiegeln – sind vor allem die Rahmenbereiche präzise abgebildet und in ihrem ganzen noch erhaltenen Detailreichtum erkennbar, ebenso die Struktur gebenden Elemente der Komposition.

Mit der Gesamtkomposition möchte ich auch meine Besprechung beginnen. Ich habe bereits eingangs bewusst von einer „komplexen Rahmenkonstruktion" gesprochen, da ich diese Gesamtstruktur als komprimierte Darstellung der Einheit von *mūrti* (Kultbild) und *mandir* (Tempel) verstehe. Klammern wir die zentralen Figuren aus, so können wir leicht unterschiedliche Elemente aus

1 Siehe DEVA 1991 für eine Beschreibung des von ihm auf den Anfang des 8. Jahrhunderts datierten Haupttempels, die allerdings die Nebentempel nicht erwähnt. Die besondere Attraktion des Haupttempels ist die weltbekannte, dort aufbewahrte 137 cm hohe Metallfigur einer stehenden Göttin (siehe RAWSON 1972: 92; SINGH [1983]: 65, 285 no. 116, Pl. CVIII; und OHRI 1988: 103–104, 106 Fig. 4, 107–108).

der Tempelarchitektur ausmachen. Die seitlichen, vertikalen Elemente entsprechen exakt dem klassischen Rahmenaufbau eines Tempeleingangs. Dabei tritt eine vertikale Aneinanderreihung von architektonisch gestalteten Nischen, in denen vorwiegend Figuren aus dem śivaitischen Kontext in Szene gesetzt sind, hervor. Den oberen Abschluss bildet auf beiden Seiten ein Nāgara-Tempel mit seiner typischen Portalarchitektur und dem darüber hochragenden Śikhara-Turm. Dieses hervorstechende Element befindet sich zwischen zwei Reihen von gehörnten Mischwesen, die wahlweise aus Elefant, Löwe und Greif zusammengesetzt sind.

Abb. 3 3D-Modell der Stele. Die Perspektive von oben verdeutlicht die Dreidimensionalität des Objekts und die Rücksprünge im Aufbau

Den oberen mittleren Abschluss der Stele bildet ein bogenförmiges Element, das an die tonnenförmige Dachform eines Valabhī-Tempels erinnert. Auch hier befindet sich mittig die Abbildung eines Tempels, wobei über dem Portalbereich nur der *śukanāsa* (Frontispiz) mit zentralem *gavākṣa* deutlich zu sehen ist. Darüber folgt ein *āmalaka* mit bekrönendem *stūpī*, wobei die übliche Vasenform dieses Elements hier eventuell als Śiva-*liṅgam* erscheint (aufgrund zu weniger Aufnahmen im Modell nicht generiert). Größe von *āmalaka* und *stūpī/liṅgam* sind ein eindeutiges Indiz dafür, dass sich ihre Funktion als oberer Abschluss auf die gesamte Stele bezieht. Wir haben es meiner Meinung nach hier insgesamt mit der komprimierten Darstellung eines Śiva-Tempels zu tun, wobei die Künstler die wichtigsten Komponenten der Tempelarchitektur in verkleinerter Form neu konfigurierten und gleichzeitig die Dreidimensionalität einer Architektur in die Zweidimensionalität einer Stele übersetzten. So betrachtet kann auch die achtblättrige Lotos-Rosette, die mittig im Zentralfeld sehr detailreich herausgearbeitet wurde, als in die Vertikale geklapptes Deckenmotiv angesehen werden. Die Lotosblume ist als klassisches Deckenelement in jedem indischen Tempel zu finden,[2] erscheint auf Kultstelen aber auch häufig als Nimbus direkt hinter dem Kopf der dargestellten Gottheit.[3] Hier steht die Lotosblume im Zentrum des *garbhagṛha*, des innersten Heiligtums. Sie ist damit dem zentralen Kultbild, in diesem Fall Umāmaheśvara, direkt zugeordnet (**Abb. 5**). Nur mittels „Herein-klappen" in die Ansichtsebene ist diese elementare Verbindung aus der gebauten Architektur in der frontalen Ansicht der Stele wiederzugeben.

Damit wären alle entscheidenden Elemente der Sakralarchitektur vorhanden: Portal mit Rahmen, Tempeldach, *āmalaka* mit *stūpī/liṅgam*, und sogar die Lotusdecke. Dieser Ansatz der Adaption einer idealen, hier śivaitischen Sakralarchitektur für die Bildkunst ist vergleichbar mit Darstellungen des Mahābodhi-Tempels auf Stelen der Pāla- und Sena-Zeit im östlichen Indien.[4] Auch dort wurden die charakteristischen Merkmale der konkreten Architektur in eine reduzierte, zweidimensionale Bildsprache übertragen. Was die Umāmaheśvara-Stele jedoch von den Mahābodhi-Stelen und nach meinem momentanen Wissensstand auch von allen anderen hinduistischen Stelen unterscheidet, ist, dass sie aus mehreren Einzelkomponenten zusammengefügt ist. Anhand des Modells lässt sich auf jeden Fall eine durchgehende

2 Siehe z. B. Wessels-Mevissen 2016.

3 Siehe z. B. Singh [1983]: Pls. LXXXVIII, LXXXIX(b), XC(a), XCIII, CIII(b); Donaldson 2007, Vol. 2: Figs. C-13, C-27, C-91, C-95, C-113, C-124, C-133, C-145–147, C-149, C-155, C-163–165, 8, 11, 13–14, 16, 42, 52, 87. 109–110, 122–123, 225, 267, 298, 324, 349, 364, 371, 396, 398–402, 410, 421, 428, 482, 484, 486–489, 491–492, 496, 502, 538, 543, 545–548, 554, 560, 562, 567.

4 Zum Aufbau einer Mahābodhi-Tempeldarstellung siehe Kozicz & Poell 2021: 72–76, Figs. 2, 4 und 11.

Abb. 4 Orthogonale (entzerrte) Ansicht des 3D-Modells

Fuge zwischen dem Zentralfeld und dem oberen „Valabhī-Element" ausmachen (siehe **Abb. 7**). Der Zusammenhalt der beiden kann nur durch die seitlichen Rahmenfelder erfolgen. Diese müssen dazu logischerweise von außen mittels Steckverbindungen hinzugefügt werden. Damit ergeben sich mindestens vier Einzelkomponenten. Konstruktiv betrachtet stellt die Stele somit einen Portalrahmen dar. Sie ist gleichzeitig Architektur und Skulptur. Ob auch die beiden Hauptgottheiten ein eigenes Element bilden, das vor die Lotos-Rosette gestellt wurde, lässt sich leider am 3D-Modell nicht verifizieren. Die Art und Weise, wie die Köpfe nur knapp vor der Rückenplatte rundum und die Lotosform dahinter gearbeitet wurden, berechtigt zumindest zu dieser Annahme.

Nun zu den Gottheiten selbst. Deutlich ist der Größenunterschied zwischen Śiva und Pārvatī, der sich durch die Körpersprache verstärkt. Der vierarmige Śiva scheint geradezu lässig mit einem linken Ellbogen auf der Schulter seiner Gemahlin zu lehnen, die unter dem Druck sich leicht zu ihm zu neigen scheint. Śiva ist dreiköpfig, eine eher ungewöhnliche Form in der gemeinsamen Darstellung, worauf bereits Donaldson ausdrücklich hingewiesen hat.[5] Śivas Hauptkopf trägt eine dreizackige Krone und ist wesentlich größer als die beiden seitlichen. In der äußeren rechten Hand hält er den Dreizack (*triśūla*), in der inneren Rechten eine Gebetskette (*akṣamālā*). Śivas innere linke Hand umfasst einen Flakon, während die äußere über Pārvatīs Kopfschmuck eine Schlange hochhält. Die Göttin ist weitgehend verhüllt. Ihre Körperform und die breite Blumengirlande lassen sich nur als Umrisse nach dem Foto aus den 1980er-Jahren rekonstruieren – ebenso die untere Körperhälfte Śivas. Nur der Bulle, Śivas Reittier, lugt hinter dem textilen Beinkleid hervor. Die Lotos-Rosette im Hintergrund wird von zwei Vidyādharas, fliegenden himmlischen Wesenheiten,[6] sowie zwei Miniatur-Tempeln flankiert. Darin ist jeweils eine vierarmige, sitzende Figur zu sehen, ein Bein

---

[5] Donaldson (2007, Vol. 1: 325) listet vier weitere mit Pārvatī dargestellte, stehende dreiköpfige Śivas, einen aus Chamba (*ibid.*, Vol. 2: Fig. 277) und drei aus der Nachbarregion Kaschmir (*ibid.*, Vol. 2: Figs. C-94, 274, 275). Eine vergleichbare Umāmaheśvara-Stele ist im Gaurīśaṅkara-Tempel von Jagatsukh, Kulu, erhalten (Kozicz 2019: 135–136, Figs. 7, 8, 9).

[6] Vidyādharas sind auch um die zentralen Lotosblumen der Holzdecke des Śaktidevī-Tempels (siehe Deva 1991, Vol. 2: Pl. 207) und anderen frühen Decken in der Region zu finden. Sie sind Bestandteil des ikonographischen Systems einer Decke.

Abb. 5 Die Lotosblume als Zentrum der umgebenden, architektonischen Rahmenkonstruktion

Abb. 6 Das bogenförmige Valabhī-Element mit dahinter aufragendem Āmalaka mit Stūpī/Liṅgam

eingeschlagen, das andere nach unten abgewinkelt, während eine Hand jeweils eine grüßende Geste in Richtung Bildzentrum ausführt. Der obere Aufbau dieser Tempel ist ähnlich dem zentralen Tempel im „Valabhī-Feld" darüber (**Abb. 6**). Letzterer ist für das Programm der Stele von besonderer Bedeutung. Unabhängig davon, ob man es als zentrales Feld des architektonischen Gesamtportals oder als Mittelfeld des Türrahmens betrachtet, die darin abgebildete Figur steht in direktem Bezug zum Programm der Stele und bringt dieses auf den Punkt.

Es ist trotz Abnutzung leicht erkennbar, dass es sich hier um einen achtarmigen und vierbeinigen, tanzenden Śiva handeln muss. Von den Attributen sind am besten die Schale, der Dreizack und die Handtrommel erhalten. Flankiert wird er zur Rechten von einem vierarmigen Indra, der durch das *vajra* (Diamantzepter) in der unteren linken Hand und den Elefanten als Reittier eindeutig identifizierbar ist. Zur Linken ist Sūrya mit vier Armen abgebildet, deutlich zu erkennen an den beiden spitz zulaufenden Lotosblumen sowie an der Löwenstandarte. Das horizontal vor der Körpermitte getragene Kurzschwert ist charakteristisch für den kaschmirischen Einfluss.[7] Bei den beiden kleinen Nebenfiguren kann es sich nur um Piṅgala und Daṇḍin handeln.

Es bleiben nun noch die Szenen in den Nischen der vertikalen Rahmenelemente. Sie sind ebenfalls teilweise unkenntlich, jedoch könnte eine gewisse „Bedeutungssymmetrie" im Gesamtaufbau in einigen Fällen Hinweise zur Identifikation liefern (**Abb. 7**). Die erste Szene rechts oben – aus Sicht des Betrachters – zeigt die Hochzeit von Śiva und Pārvatī. Die beiden sind einander zugewandt und reichen sich die Hände über dem rituellen Hochzeitsfeuer. Im Hintergrund zeichnet sich mittig eine weitere Gestalt ab, vermutlich Himavān, der Brautvater, oder Viṣṇu, der Brautbruder. Im Feld gegenüber (2) scheint Śiva von zwei stehenden, weiblichen Figuren flankiert zu sein, zwei Vidyādharas schweben neben seinem Kopf. Aufgrund der angesprochenen Symmetrie wäre naheliegend, die beiden stehenden Figuren als die beiden Gemahlinnen Śivas, nämlich Satī/Pārvatī und die Flussgöttin Gaṅgā, zu identifizieren.[8] Die Figur darunter (3) kann aufgrund der Ausformung der linken Brust wohl als Ardhanārīśvara, die Vereinigungsform von Śiva und Pārvatī, identifiziert werden (**Abb. 8**).

Gegenüber auf der rechten Seite der Stele (4) ist ein dreiköpfiger Maheśvara abgebildet, vor dem ein Liṅgam aufgebaut scheint. Die Szene darunter (5) zeigt den Asura (Dämon) Andhaka, wie er von Śiva im Ausfallschritt mit dem Dreizack aufgespießt wird. Sehr ähnlich ist das Thema in der Nische links gegenüber (6), wo eine etwas dickbäuchige Form Śivas ein am Boden befindliches Objekt aufspießt. Die Körperform deutet auf Bhairava hin, die zornvolle und mit dem Tod assoziierte Form Śivas. Um eine andere Form Bhairavas handelt es sich mit hoher Wahrscheinlichkeit bei der Figur darunter (7), die mit dem Dreizack zum Schlag ausholt und eine Schlange quer vor dem Körper hält (**Abb. 9**). Auf Bhairava deutet auch hier die Korpulenz, vor allem aber der Leichnam unter den Füßen hin. Gegenüber auf der rechten Seite (8) steht wieder eine vierarmige, dreiköpfige Figur (**Abb. 10**). Śi-

7 Siehe Shah 2021: 112–115 und Figs. 1–4, 11–12, 16.

8 Zu den zwei Hochzeiten Śivas siehe Bhattacharya 2004–05.

Abb. 7 Nachzeichnung. Die Nummerierung der Szenen entspricht der Reihenfolge in der Beschreibung

Abb. 8 Ardhanārīśvara in einer miniaturisierten Tempelnische mit kaschmirischem Giebel

Abb. 9 Bhairava, darunter Gaṇeśa

vas Dreizack in der Rechten zeichnet sich klar ab; darunter sieht man auch deutlich Kopf und Beine des Bullen. Die Attribute in den linken Händen sind unklar. Einen Hinweis auf die Identität bietet jedoch der längliche, spitz zulaufende linke Kopf. Die Figur müsste Hari-Hara sein, die Mischform aus Śiva und Viṣṇu. Der linke Kopf wäre demnach der Kopf des Eber-Avatāra Viṣṇus (Varāha). Die unkenntliche Figur unten neben der Viṣṇu-Seite (auf der Zeichnung nicht wiedergegeben) wäre dann Garuḍa, Viṣṇus Reittier. In Bezug auf die Gesamtkomposition ist festzuhalten, dass die vier vierarmigen Darstellungen (3/4 und 7/8) sich paarweise gegenüberstehen – und zwar in jenen Nischen, die sich von den anderen durch einen darübergesetzten, an die Architektur Kaschmirs angelehnten Dreiecksgiebel unterscheiden (siehe **Abb. 7**). Symmetrie in Bezug auf Szeneninhalt und Thema sowie gestalterischer Rhythmus zeichnen sich als bestimmende Faktoren für die Anordnung ab. Die unterste Figur im linken Rahmen (9) zeigt Gaṇeśa. Die gegenüberliegende Figur (10) zeichnet sich durch korpulenten Körperbau, Zweiarmigkeit und Dreizack aus. Die Identifikation als Skanda-Kumāra, Sohn Śivas, ergibt sich sowohl aus dem Dreizack (eigentlich Speer) als auch durch die Paarung mit Gaṇeśa. Die Söhne Śivas bilden damit den unteren Abschluss. Ikonographisch stellt die Stele eine Übersicht über das śivaitische Pantheon dar.

Abb. 10 Hari-Hara, darunter Skanda-Kumāra

Dieser Aufsatz stellt eine erste Bestandsaufnahme jener Fakten und auch Vermutungen dar, die sich aus der analytischen Betrachtung des 3D-Modells ergeben. Das Modell erlaubt Heranzoomen und Rotation, und damit Einblicke, die gerade in diesem Fall, wo das Betreten des Kultraums nicht gestattet ist, wissenschaftliches Arbeiten überhaupt erst ermöglichen. Qualitativ kommt das 3D-Modell der Umāmaheśvara-Stele nahe an jene aus Museumsbeständen heran. Lückenlos werden Modelle von Objekten, die in ihrem ursprünglichen rituellen und räumlichen Kontext dokumentiert werden, wohl selten sein. Dafür bestechen sie mit der Aura des Authentischen. 3D-Modelle können auch dazu dienen, dokumentierte Objekte und deren Zustand nachhaltig zu archivieren, und damit einen bedeutsamen Beitrag zur Erhaltung der Kulturgüter leisten. Die Weiterführung eines solchen Modells in VR (virtual reality) oder AR (augmented reality) ist nur der nächste logische Schritt – ein Schritt, der diese Objekte auch in einer Museumsumgebung erlebbar machen könnte.

Danksagung

Dieser Artikel wurde im Rahmen zweier vom österreichischen Fonds zur Förderung der wissenschaftlichen Forschung geförderten Projekte (P28509 und P32131) am Institut für Architektur und Medien der TU Graz erarbeitet. Das 3D-Modell (Abb. 3, 4) und die Renderings wurden von meinem Kollegen Max Frühwirt generiert. Alle anderen Abbildungen stammen vom Autor. Mein besonderer Dank geht an Gerd Mevissen für das sorgfältige Editieren und die exakten Korrekturen, und vor allem die ergänzenden Quellenhinweise.

Bibliographie

Bhattacharya, Gouriswar (2004–05) The Two Marriages of Śiva. *Journal of Bengal Art* (Dhaka) 9&10, 2004–2005 [publ. 2007]: 247–256.

Deva, Krishna (1991) Chatrārhi, Śakti temple. *Encyclopaedia of Indian Temple Architecture. Vol. II, Part 2: North India. Period of Early Maturity, c. A.D. 700–900*, eds. M.W. Meister & M.A. Dhaky. 2 volumes. New Delhi: 101–102, Fig. 46 & Pls. 204–211.

Donaldson, Thomas Eugene (2007) *Śiva-Pārvatī and Allied Images: Their Iconography and Body Language*. 2 Volumes. New Delhi.

Kozicz, Gerald (2019) Embedded in Living Tradition: The Gaurishankar Shrine of Jagatsukh. *Orientations* (Hong Kong) 50/5: 130–136.

Kozicz, Gerald & Heinrich Poell (2021) The Dharmarajika Stele Revisited. *Orientations* (Hong Kong) 52/2: 71–77.

Ohri, Vishwa Chander (1988) Hill Bronzes from the Chamba Area. *The Great Tradition: Indian Bronze Masterpieces*, ed. Asha Rani Mathur. New Delhi: 102–115.

Postel M., N. Neven & K. Mankodi (1985) *Antiquities of Himachal*. Bombay.

Rawson, Philip (1972) *Indian Art*. London.

Shah, Ibrahim (2021) Three Kashmiri Sūrya Images in the Lahore Museum, Pakistan: Artistic and Iconographic Considerations. *Berliner Indologische Studien* (Berlin) 25: 97–121.

Singh, Mian Goverdhan [1983] *Art and Architecture of Himachal Pradesh*. Delhi (not dated).

Wessels-Mevissen, Corinna (2016) A Note on the Ceiling Designs in the Temples of Northern Karnataka, with Special Emphasis on the Lotus Blossom Motif. *Temple Architecture and Imagery of South and Southeast Asia. Prāsādanidhi: Papers presented to Professor M.A. Dhaky*, eds. Parul Pandya Dhar & Gerd J.R. Mevissen. New Delhi: 123–137 & col.pl. 11.

English Summary

The Śaktidevī of Chatrarhi is famous for its wooden portal and the metal statue of a female deity (Devī) datable to the 8th century. Lesser known and rarely published is a stone sculpture of Umāmaheśvara, i.e. Śiva (Śaṅkara) and Pārvatī (Gaurī). The celestial couple is depicted in a standing position in the center of an elaborate frame. Structurally, this frame is a multi-frame composition, the components of which are assembled like the jambs and lintels of a door frame. It displays all the elements of a true architectural shrine: a *valabhī* element as the central super-structure topped by an *āmalaka* with *stūpī/liṅgam*, two flanking *nāgara* temples on top of the lateral jambs and a lotus rosette behind the heads of the celestial couple. The jambs display scenes and deities related to the śaiva pantheon. This article features the documentation and discussion of the stele using photogrammetry-based 3D-models. It is a case-study of state-of-the-art technology in field research that enabled us to study and present an object which is otherwise not accessible since access to the sanctum is not allowed nowadays.

Religious Transfer from India to the Mekong Delta – Three Different Cases Documented by Images

Adalbert J. Gail

Religious images are both symbols and carriers of religious ideas. Their role as important documents of beliefs is even more important, if other witnesses such as texts or inscription are rare or even missing.

In the first centuries of our era, we notice a striking religious transfer from India to Southeast Asia (Cœdès 1968: 14–35). The Mekong delta seems to have had overwhelming importance as some sort of relay station, from where Hindu as well as Buddhist ideas migrated onwards both mainland and island Southeast Asia.

Particulars of that process, that can be interpreted as a partial acculturation[1] have not been reported. It is plausible, however, that Indian trading posts in the Mekong delta grew into establishments that comprised religious institutions and represented somehow „little India“ abroad.

Fig. 1 Sūrya from Oc Eo, Southern Vietnam, stone, ca. 7th century; Museum of Vietnam History, Hoh Chi Minh City. Photo: Wikimedia commons/dederot

Our first example is the Indian sun god Sūrya. From the Mekong delta (Oc Eo[2], South Vietnam) we know of two, and from the Si The province in Central Thailand we know of three, figurative stone representations of Sūrya (Guy 2019: Cat. 68–70), which are sculpted in the round and are tall enough – the fragments are between 85 and 108 cm high – to let us think not just of a domestic sun cult but of public worship of the sun god (**Fig. 1**).

The singular outfit of Sūrya strongly reminds us of the North Indian iconography of Sūrya that originated during the Kuṣāṇa period in Mathurā (UP) and was prevalent in the following centuries (**Fig. 2**).

Several textual references make clear that the Indian sun cult was established by sun priests who came from Iran. The developed legend of the Sāmba-Purāṇa (ca. 5th c. CE) skilfully connects Iranian origin with Mathurā's Kṛṣṇaism. Accordingly, Sāmba, son of Kṛṣṇa, brought Maga families from *Śakadvīpa* (Sistan) to India and founded the earliest sun temple in *Mūlasthāna* (Multan, Pakistan; Stietencron 1966: 125–142; Gail 2010: 154). Two sources (*Bṛhatsaṃhitā* 58, 46 and *Viṣṇudharmottara-Purāṇa* 67,2) mention Sūrya's typical outfit, the long tunic and boots[3], called northern apparel (*udīcyaveṣa*).

For the purposes of our investigation, I have selected three characteristic figurative representations of gods whose place of origin, India, is beyond doubt. That does not mean that the artefacts are manufactured in India. More reasonable is the assumption that they were made in Southeast Asia, but their Indian ancestry is quite evident. These sculptures are able to function as reliable guides to the migration of religious ideas.

1 Basic features of the Indian society as the caste system never characterised the Southeast Asian societies.

2 Oc Eo is an important site of archaeological findings in the Mekong delta.

3 Fig. 1 seems to have had short boots.

Fig. 2 Sūrya, gavākṣa of Bhumara temple, India, stone, ca. 5th century; Indian Museum Kolkata. Photo: www.wikipedia.org/ Biswarup Ganguly

A theoretical updating of this legend would run as follows: Having established sun temples in India, Sāmba thought that the sun cult should also be established in other countries, where Indian cults already flourished. So, he selected sun priests, who accompanied merchants to the Mekong delta and other places in Mainland Southeast Asia. Indigenous craftsmen here sculpted figures of the sun god that followed North Indian models, particularly the *udīcyaveṣa* and lotus buds in Sūrya's two hands.

In fact, we have no record of how the sun cult came to Mainland Southeast Asia. The sculptures prove the migration not only of religious but also of iconographic ideas.

The nearest relative of the Kuṣāṇa models seems to be one of the Oc Eo figures (102 cm high), whose robe falls straight and widens towards the lower hem (**Fig. 1**)[4].

The fate of the Southeast Asian sun cult, however, seems not to have been a happy one. From the early Angkorean period onwards (802 CE) we do not find any larger representations of Sūrya, nor any temple dedicated to the sun, not even side shrines. Sun worship survived only within the group of the Nine Planets (*navagraha,* **Fig. 3**).

Now let us turn to the female deity Durgā. From the 7th century CE onwards figures of Durgā are known that stand on the severed head of the buffalo *Mahiṣāsura,* in the Mekong delta as well as in southern Cambodia (Guy 2019: Cat. 66) (**Fig. 4**). Here Mahiṣa is carved into the base of the figure. Together with other sculptures Durgā was also found in Hindu sanctuaries, discovered in the ruins of Oc Eo (Le Thi Lien 2014: 119). This type of Durgā definitely did not reach the Mekong delta from North India in the way Sūrya and the Saura cult did, but from the Dravidian south. The evidence suggests that this icon is characteristic of both areas. In the Mekong delta as well as in Tamil Nadu the depiction focuses on the narrative moment: Durgā *after* the defeat of the buffalo demon (**Fig. 5**)[5].

What was the function of Durgā *victrix* in the Pallava realm, exported from the Coromadel coast via the Indian Ocean to the Mekong delta? Did she represent the Indian *Śakti* cult – her defeat of Mahiṣāsura de facto means the supremacy of female over male power – or was she just a ferocious aspect of Śiva's wife Umā and as such integrated into the basic Śiva cult? A few facts seem to plead in favour of the former assumption. In Māmallapuram the Draupadī *ratha* is a Durgā temple with three (partly incomplete) reliefs of Durgā on the outer walls, where she is depicted in precisely that attitude described above (**Fig. 6**). Inside on the back wall there is a cult image of Durgā on a lotus socle; on her right side kneels a warrior committing ritual suicide (**Fig. 7**)[6]. Next to the Trimūrti cave in Māmallapuram, dedicated to Śiva, Skanda as Brahmaśāstā and Viṣṇu (Srinivasan 1964: 159), is a separate niche for the eight-armed Durgā standing on the

Fig. 3 Navagraha lintel from Angkor, sandstone, ca. 10th Century; National Museum, Pnomh Penh. Photo: Angkor 2007: Kat. No. 48

4 Yet incised decorative folds seem to 'falsify' this impression, since they turn the tunic into a pleated gown.

5 In North India the combat itself is the subject of most Durgā depictions.

6 J. P. Vogel 1930–32 collected five instances of reliefs from the Pallava period where soldiers commit suicide in front of Durgā, thus giving thanks to their goddess of victory. See also Filliozat 1968.

Fig. 4 Durgā, Prä-Angkor ca. 7th century; National Museum, Phnom Penh. Photo: A.J. Gail

Fig. 5 Durgā, south of Trimūrti maṇḍapa Māmallapuram, India, 7th century. Photo: A.J. Gail

Fig. 6 Draupadīratha from northwest, Māmallapuram, India, 7th century. Photo: A.J. Gail

Mahiṣa head (**Fig. 5**).[7] These observations seem to plead for a *śakti* cult by the Pallavas, a cult that was exported to the Mekong area. The iconographical features of the early Southeast Asian Durgā more or less copied the Pallava model (**Fig. 5**)[8].

Once more we try to trace the fate of an early Durgā/Śakti cult (7th/8th centuries CE) in the Angkorean period of Mainland Southeast Asia (802 onwards). Indeed, we do not find – among hundreds of temples – a single temple where Durgā was worshipped as the main deity. Moreover, there is no main temple dedicated to Devī.[9] Two of three Sancta of Banteay Srei are dedicated to Śiva, one to Viṣṇu, not to Devī/Śakti (GLAIZE 1993: 231). The Śakti cult, in India a main branch of Hinduism, is absent from the map of cults among the Khmer.[10]

The disappearance of the icon *Durgā standing on the head of Mahiṣa* in the 9th century CE symbolically attests the disappearance of the early Śakti cult on the way from the Mekong delta to the region of Angkor.[11]

In Champa this Durga type is represented by just one single specimen (BAPTISTE/ZÉPHIR 2005: Cat. 31). The Cham worshipped their own terrestrial goddess *yāng pu nagara* (or Po Nagar), who was identified with Śiva's wife Bhagavatī in Sanskrit texts.[12]

In Angkor the importance of a female principle that imbues religious practice seems to have fundamentally changed a few centuries later. The Mahāyāna Buddhism of Jayavarman VII attributed to the goddess *Prajñā* – who

7 The spectacular Mahiṣamardinī cave shows on a large scale Durgā defeating the anthropomorphic Mahiṣa. The relief covers the whole northern wall of the *maṇḍapa* (SRINIVASAN 1964: 154f., Pl. XLVII). The northern one of the three sancta (SRINIVASAN, op. cit., Fig. 30) might have been dedicated to Durgā. In combination with the Anantaśayana relief that covers the south wall of the *maṇḍapa* it has convincingly been argued that the two reliefs follow the *Devīmāhātmya*, which is, *notabene*, an important Śāktic text (SRINIVASAN, op. cit.: 155 fn. 1 and 2).

8 This observation holds good for *śaṅkha* and *cakra* carried by the upper two hands. These ‚Vaiṣṇava symbols' connect Durgā with South Indian Viṣṇu, whose sister she is according to South Indian perception.

9 A side shrine dedicated to Umā can be found among the *pañcāyatana* deities of the Pre Rup temple (see GAIL 2021).

10 "La *śakti* ...a toujours occupé, au Cambodge, une place inferieure à celle de Śiva: il n'y a pas eu de culte *śākta* proprement dit" (BHATTACHARYA 1961: 90). "...le Cambodge est resté à l'écart du grand courant śākta qui place la Déesse sur le même plan que Śiva et Viṣṇu" (DAGENS 2013: 182).

11 See the collection of Devī/Durgā figures in the National Museum of Phnom Penh: KHUN SAMÉN 2004.

12 Her main temple, larger than Śiva's, stands amidst the temple group of Po nagar of NhaTrang in Central Vietnam (SCHWEYER 2008: 179–182; 2011: 102–107).

Fig. 7 Durgā, cult relief of Draupadīratha, Māmallapuram, India. Photo: A.J. Gail

with a pinch of salt might be termed the Buddhist counterpart of the Hindu *Śakti* (Mallmann 1976: 36–38) – a significant role. The vast Ta Prohm temple was dedicated to Prajñāpāramitā (Glaize 1993: 184). This goddess forms part of the important trio Buddha, Avalokiteśvara and Prajñāpāramitā (**Fig. 8**).

Our third religious transfer that takes the god Viṣṇu into account requires a preliminary remark.

The most popular branch of Hinduism in all Southeast Asia was Śaivism, which also dominates South India. Kings often used to identify themselves with each newly erected *liṅga* by baptising them with their personal names.

Inscriptional examples include the earlier shore temple at Māmallapuram, the *Rājasiṃheśvara* named after Narasiṃhavarman II Rājasiṃha, and, demarcating the easternmost area of Hinduism, the *Bhadreśvara* after King Bhadravarman, in Champa (Central Vietnam).[13]

Since Śaivism, however, is dominated by the uniconic *liṅga* in contrast to the figurative representations of Viṣṇu, Vaiṣṇavism provides a better chance of following iconographic, i.e. historical, traces from India to Southeast Asia.

Vaiṣṇavism is present from the very beginning of inscriptional or pictorial testimonies that are pertinent to Hinduism outside India.

Viṣṇu's iconography in the delta has been a mixture of North- and South Indian elements from the 7th/8th century onwards. He is always depicted as four-armed. His upper hands – and that is the South Indian contribution – carry wheel (*cakra*) and conch (*śaṅkha*), while one of his lower hands holds a club (*gadā*), the other one the globe of the earth (*mahī*). The latter symbol is never depicted in South India. Pallava depictions of Viṣṇu with *śaṅkha* and *cakra* can be traced from the 7th century onwards, the earliest specimens *in situ* be-

Fig. 8 Buddhist Triad from Roluos, Siem Reap, Cambodia, Bronze, 12th/13th century; National Museum, Pnomh Penh. Photo: Angkor 2007: Kat. No. 82

13 Meister 1983: 53–56. Schweyer 2011: 177f. and passim.

Fig. 9 Viṣṇu at Dharmarājaratha, Māmallapuram, India. Photo: A.J. Gail

Fig. 10 Viṣṇu from Allahabad, India, sandstone, ca. 5th century; Brooklyn Museum, New York, Gift of Amy and Robert L. Poster and anonymous donors, 81.203. Photo: Creative Commons-BY Brooklyn Museum, 81.203_PS2.jpg

Fig. 11 Viṣṇu from Mathura, India, red sandstone, ca. 3rd; Museum für Asiatische Kunst Berlin, Inv.-Nr. I 5878. Photo: Staatliche Museen zu Berlin, Museum für Asiatische Kunst / Iris Papadopoulos

ing in Māmallapuram, Dharmarājaratha (**Fig. 9**), in the southern niche of the three Trimūrtimaṇḍapa niches and in the Ādivarāhamaṇḍapa (Srinivasan 1962: 160, 170 and pl. LIII A). Viṣṇu carrying the earth-globe is represented by a figure from Allahabad, dated to the early 5th century (Gail 2020: 20; **Abb. 10**). The club is also a northern contribution, beginning with early Viṣṇu images from Mathurā (**Fig. 11**).

A combination of these four attributes – the conch undoubtedly held in the upper left is lost – forms part of a spectacular figure of Viṣṇu (7th–8th century) excavated in 1998 in the Mekong delta, Dong Thap province (**Fig. 12**). Here we also come upon "a series of substantial sanctuaries devoted to the cult of Viṣṇu in the region" (Guy 2014: Cat. 59)[14].

Many of the later images are based on this example. It is the main type symbolizing a Viṣṇu cult that conquers the whole mainland and several islands of Southeast Asia, often side by side with the worship of Śiva (**Fig. 13**). The specimens from Eastern Java and Champa show Viṣṇu with the earth-globe in one of his lower hands and seated on his vehicle, the king of birds Garuḍa (see Gail in this periodical 24/2020: 20–24, Abb. 4 and 5).[15]

Conclusion

We tried to trace three Hindu religions that were exported from India to the Mekong delta in mainland Southeast Asia. These are the Sauras, the Śāktas and the Vaiṣṇavas. The models we used were typical sculptures that seem to have been manufactured using Indian specimens and that could have functioned as cult icons of the respective religions. While the Sūrya figures are doubtless sculpted after North Indian models, where the Saura cult orig-

14 An *in situ* photo taken during excavation can be found in Khoo 2003: 36.

15 An interesting difference is the attitude (*āsana*) of Garuḍa. The Java figure shows him in the 'Buddhist' *vajraparyaṅka/padmāsana* posture, the Champa sculpture according to an old tradition in kneeling position.

inated, the Durgā sculptures breathe a South Indian spirit, and the figure of four-armed Viṣṇu (with *cakra* and *śaṅkha* in the upper hands, club and earth globe in the lower hands) combines North- and South Indian influences.

The Saura religion seems to have lacked successors to the Indian sun priests, who came from India on a Northern route – most probably via Gaṅgā and the Bengal Sea – to the Mekong delta (and Central Thailand).

The Indian Śakti cult, that is to say the Śākta religion, became integrated into overall Śiva worship. This seems evident regarding the vast Khmer empire. The Cham created and worshipped an indigenous terrestrial goddess.

The Viṣṇu religion, however, persisted and flourished from the very beginning down to the disappearance of Hindu cults in Mainland Southeast Asia.

Fig. 12 Viṣṇu from Dong Thap, Southern Vietnam, stone, ca. 7th/8th century; Dong Thap Province Museum, Vietnam. Photo: GUY 2014: No. 59

BIBLIOGRAPHY

Angkor. Göttliches Erbe Kambodschas. 15.12.2006–9.4.2007 Kunst- und Ausstellungshalle der Bundesrepublik Deutschland, Bonn. Berlin: Prestel.

BAPTISTE, Pierre / ZÉPHIR, Thierry, eds. (2005) *Trésor d'art du Vietnam. La Sculpture du Champa Ve–XVe siècles.* Paris: Éditions de la Réunion des musées nationaux.

BHATTACHARYA, Kamaleswar (1961) *Les Religions Brahmaniques dans l'Ancien Cambodge.* Paris: École Française d'Extrême-Orient.

CŒDÈS, George (1968) *The Indianized States of Southeast Asia.* Ed. Walter F. Vella. Translated by Sue Brown Coing. Honolulu: University of Hawai Press [Translated from George Coedès 1964. *Les États hindouisés d'Indochine et d'Indonésie, nouvelle édition revue et mise à jour.* Paris: Éditions E. De Boccard.]

DAGENS, Bruno (2013) *Les Khmers.* Paris: Éditions Les Belles Lettres.

DALLAPICCOLA, Anna L. and Anila VERGHESE eds. (2017) *India and Southeast Asia: Cultural Discourses.* Mumbai: The K R Oriental Institute, Mumbai.

FILLIOZAT, Jean (1968) L'abandon de la vie par le sage et les suicides du criminel et du héros dans la tradition indienne. *Arts Asiatiques* (Paris)15, 74–88.

GAIL, Adalbert J. (2001) *Sonnenkult in Indien. Tempel und Skulpturen von den Anfängen bis zur Gegenwart.* Berlin: Reimer.

— (2010) Armed and Booted. Sun god and sun cult in Hinduism. *Sun Worship in the Civilizations of the World.* Ed. Adalbert J. Gail. Prague: Special Issue *Pandanus* '10 4/2: 153–171.

— (2020) Viṣṇu und die kosmographische Revolution. *Indo-Asiatische Zeitschrift* 24: 20–24.

— (2021) Pre Rup and the Mātṛkās. *Jñāna Pravāha. Research Journal* No. XXIV: 1–7, 10 Figures.

GLAIZE, Maurice (1993) *Les Monuments du Groupe d'Angkor.* Paris: J. Maisonneuve.

GUY, John ed. (2014) *Lost Kingdoms. Hindu-Buddhist Sculpture of Early Southeast Asia.* New York: The Metropolitan Museum of Art, New York.

KHOO, James C.M. ed. (2003) *Art & Archaeology of Fu Nan. Pre-Khmer Kingdom of the Lower Mekong Valley.* Bangkok: The Southeast Asian Ceramic Society.

KHUN SAMÉN (2007) *Preah Néang Tévi. Collections du Musée National Phnom Penh.* Phnom Penh: Imprimerie Ariyathoar.

MEISTER, Michael W. (1983) ed. *Encyclopaedia of Indian Temple Architecture. South India. Lower Drāviḍadeśa 200 BC – AD 1324*: American Institute of Indian Studies / University of Pennsylvania Press.

LE THI LIEN (2014) Hindu-Buddhist Sculpture in Southern Vietnam: Evolution of Icons and Styles to the Eighth Century. Guy, John ed. 2014. *Lost Kingdoms. Hindu-Buddhist Sculpture of Early Southeast Asia,*

Fig. 13 Viṣṇu in Bayon gallery, Angkor Thom, 13th century. Photo: A.J. Gail

118–121. New York: The Metropolitain Museum of Art, New York.

MALLMANN, Marie-Therèse (1976). *Introduction a l'Iconographie du Tântrisme Bouddhique*. Paris: Librairie Adrien-Maisonneuve.

SCHWEYER, Anne-Valérie (2008) *Le Viêtnam Ancien*. Paris: Les Belles Lettres.

— (2011) *Ancient Vietnam. History, Art and Archaeology*. Bangkok: River Books.

SHAH, Priyabala ed. (1958) *Viṣṇudharmottara-Purāṇa. Third Khaṇḍa*. Two vols. text and translation. Baroda. Oriental Institute.

SRINIVASAN, K.R. (1964) *Cave-Temples of the Pallavas*. New Delhi: Archaeological Survey of India.

STIETENCRON, Heinrich von (1966) *Indische Sonnenpriester. Sāmba und die Śākadvipīya-Brāhmaṇa*. Wiesbaden: Harrassowitz.

Varāhamihira (1880) *Bṛhatsaṃhitā*. Ed. Jibananda Vidyasagara. Calcutta: Sarasvatīyantra.

VOGEL, J.P. (1930–32) The Head-offering to the Goddess in Pallava Sculpture. *Bulletin of the School of Oriental Studies* 6: 539–543.

Deutsche Zusammenfassung

Das Mekongdelta scheint ein wichtiger Handelsplatz Indiens in Südostasien gewesen zu sein, wie sich aus der Präsenz indischer religiöser Kulte unschwer folgern lässt. Das Delta fungierte in einigen Fällen aber auch als diejenige Region, von der aus sich ausweislich der hier gefundenen religiösen Skulpturen indische religiöse Ideen in den weiteren südostasiatischen Raum verbreiteten. Drei ikonographisch signifikante Typen hinduistischer Skulpturen eignen sich für unsere Beobachtungen in besonderer Weise.

Als erstes Beispiel dienen Kultfiguren des Sonnengottes Sūrya, die eindeutig auf nordindische Herkunft verweisen – Stiefel als nördliche Bekleidung, *udīcyveṣa* – und Zeugnisse der Saura-Religion darstellen. Dieser Kult aber verliert sich, er ist im Khmerreich und in Champa nicht mehr nachweisbar. Der Durgā-Kult war wohl wie bei den südindischen Pallavas, ausgewiesen durch die auf dem abgeschlagenen Büffelkopf stehende Durgā, zunächst eine eigenständige Religion (Śākta), wird aber bei den Khmer in den Śiva-Kult eingeschmolzen. Endlich haben wir den Viṣṇu-Kult, dessen Präsenz über alle Perioden und Regionen Südostasiens hinweg – d.h. bis zum völligen Niedergang des Hinduismus – sichtbar ist. Auffällig ist vor allem der vierarmige Typus mit der Erde als Kugel in einer Hand. Vom Mekongdelta aus wandert er ebenso ins Khmerreich wie nach Java und Zentralvietnam.

Ein neuer Player in Dahlem – Der Forschungscampus der SPK

Alexis von Poser & Patricia Rahemipour

Die vier Begriffe „Kulturen – Forschen – Dinge – Wissen“ bilden das Koordinatensystem für einen Forschungs- und Präsentationsort neuen Typs: den Forschungscampus Dahlem. Ihn zeichnet das sparten- und sammlungsübergreifende Zusammenwirken verschiedener Institutionen der Stiftung Preußischer Kulturbesitz aus. Dazu zählen das Ethnologische Museum, das Museum für Asiatische Kunst, das Museum Europäischer Kulturen, das Institut für Museumsforschung, die Kunstbibliothek, das Rathgen-Forschungslabor der Staatlichen Museen zu Berlin sowie das Ibero-Amerikanische Institut. Vertreten werden sie durch ihre zwei Sprecher. Eine solche Struktur ist ein Novum innerhalb der Stiftung und schöpft erstmals das im Verbund angelegte Potential der Multidisziplinarität voll aus. Gemeinsam im direkten Austausch mit unterschiedlichen Partner*innen werden Projekte angestoßen und entwickelt. So besteht in diesem Zusammenhang seit 2020 eine strategische Partnerschaft mit der Freien Universität Berlin und ebenfalls seit 2020 eine enge Zusammenarbeit mit dem Fachbereich Architektur der Technischen Universität Berlin.

Im Forschungscampus Dahlem verknüpfen sich vielfältige Disziplinen, die materielle wie immaterielle Kulturen in gemeinsam entwickelten Fragestellungen erforschen und neue Formate der Wissenskommunikation nutzen. Besonders im Fokus steht dabei die Idee, Forschungs- und Erkenntnisprozesse nicht nur nachvollziehbar zu zeigen, sondern darüber hinaus auch für jede und jeden eine Teilhabe zu ermöglichen.

Grundsätzlich verfolgt der FC Dahlem mehrere Linien. Zum einen soll sammlungsbasierte Forschung transdisziplinär und unter Einbeziehung unterschiedlichster Partner vorangetrieben werden. Denn weit über 90% der Sammlungen des Ethnologischen Museums und sehr umfangreiche Bestände des Museums für Asiatische Kunst sind nicht mit ins Humboldt Forum in der Mitte Berlins umgezogen, sondern verbleiben in Dahlem. Zudem ist das Museum Europäischer Kulturen mit seinen Sammlungen und seinen innovativen Ausstellungs- und Forschungsprojekten ein zentraler Player am Standort Dahlem, beispielsweise mit dem gerade bewilligten Projekt zur kollaborativen Provenienzforschung mit Vertreter*innen der Sami. Ein wichtiger Impulsgeber für die Aktivitäten im FC Dahlem ist auch das bundesweit agierende Institut für Museumsforschung der Staatlichen Museen zu Berlin. Alle sind eingebettet in eine historisch gewachsene Forschungslandschaft, innerhalb derer vernetzt durch Partnerschaften in alle Welt die historischen Sammlungen nutzbar gemacht werden. Ein Beispiel ist in diesem Zusammenhang das Memorandum of Understanding, welches das Ethologische Museum und das Museum für Asiatische Kunst seit 2019 mit dem National Museum und der Nationalen Galerie für Moderne Kunst in New Delhi, sowie dem Indian Museum in Kolkata verbindet. Auf dessen Basis sollen gemeinsame Projekte im Bereich von Ausstellungen wie auch von Sammlungsforschung entstehen. Zudem kann hierbei auch in Fragen von Konservierung und Restaurierung ein fruchtbarer Austausch erwachsen.

Aktuell ist außerdem geplant, ein Graduiertenkolleg gemeinsam mit der Freien Universität, dem Ibero-Amerikanischen Institut und dem Ethnologischen Museum zu etablieren. Ziel des Graduiertenkollegs ist neben der Nachwuchsförderung auch die Einbindung der unterschiedlichen Perspektiven und Sammelkomplexe der Beteiligten.

In enger Verbindung mit der forschungsbasierten und transdisziplinären Sammlungsarbeit am Forschungscampus Dahlem liegt der Fokus auf dem Bereich der Wissenskommunikation. Hier werden neue Formate entwickelt in deren Zentrum die Genese und das Verhandeln von Wissen steht. Das Entstehen von Wissen hängt dabei nicht von akademischer Vorbildung ab. Es ist vielmehr ein Prozess der Aushandlung unterschiedlicher Perspek-

Eingangsbereich Lansstraße mit neuem Banner © Alexis von Poser

tiven, der hier zum Tragen kommt. Dies funktioniert nur unter Einbeziehung unterschiedlicher Disziplinen, Wissensgeber*innen und umfangreicher Teilhabe. Um dies zu veranschaulichen, wird aktuell am Forschungscampus eine Präsentation entwickelt, die sich dem Thema Zeit widmet. Zeit und Zeitwahrnehmung werden multisensorisch über Objekte, künstlerische Perspektiven, Gerüche, aber auch Musik und damit verbundene Hörerfahrungen dargestellt. Im Zentrum stehen dabei Workshops mit unterschiedlichen Interessierten, die aus ihrer sehr persönlichen Erfahrung beitragen und das Wissen um die Objekte anreichern.

Auch das architektonische Ensemble, in dem der Forschungscampus Dahlem entsteht, spielt bei seiner Entwicklung eine Rolle. So erarbeiteten Studierende des Fachbereichs Architektur der Technischen Universität Berlin Visionen zum Museumskomplex Dahlem, die den Anspruch „Kulturen – Forschen – Dinge – Wissen“ aufgreifen, umsetzbar und möglich machen.

Transdisziplinäre Zusammenarbeit und Forschung bedarf eines Rahmens, der weit über den Willen des gemeinsamen Agierens hinausgeht. Es braucht Ermöglichungsräume, die es bisher in der Stiftung Preußischer Kulturbesitz nicht gibt. Ein solcher Ermöglichungsraum wurde gerade im Vorraum des Auditoriums geschaffen. Er lädt zum Denken und Austausch ein und steht nicht nur Fachkolleg*innen, sondern auch weiteren Interessierten offen. Zunächst zweimal im Monat wird der Forschungscampus seine Türen daher öffnen und zum gemeinsamen Erdenken einladen.

Nachhaltige Partnerschaften mit internationalen Partner*innen, welche über kurze Projektphasen hinausreichen, sind ein weiteres Ziel des FC Dahlem. Dabei sollen die Prozesse der Wissensgenese im Zentrum stehen: der Forschungscampus macht Wissenschaft sichtbar und greifbar – und dies stets jenseits traditioneller Wissenshierarchien.

English Summary

At the new Forschungscampus Dahlem (Research Campus Dahlem), various institutions of the Stiftung Preussischer Kulturbesitz (Prussian Cultural Heritage Foundation) collaborate on material and immaterial cultures in a transregional perspective. The main fields of activity are research, infrastructure of knowledge and knowledge communication. It brings together diverse disciplinary, thematic and regional approaches and experiences, develops collection-based research and presents research outcomes to a broader audience. The Forschungscampus Dahlem follows the principle of making research processes transparent and enabling the participation of society at large. It is a forum for dialog among various stakeholders from science, culture, politics, business and the general public. At the same time, the Forschungscampus Dahlem views itself as the "transformation laboratory" of the SPK, a place to generate new content, formats and processes that could be important to the SPK as a whole.

Jahresrückblick 2022

Angesichts der pandemiebedingten Einschränkungen mussten alle Jours fixes seit Herbst 2021 bis zum Frühjahr 2022 wiederum digital stattfinden. Doch auch virtuell wurden die ertragreichen Vorträge von Ji Ho Yi zu den Kindern in buddhistischen Klöstern des Tarimbeckens (3. bis 7. Jh. n. Chr.), von Dr. Norbert A. Deuchert zu Aufstieg und Niedergang der Theokratie in Tibet (2. Hälfte 17. Jh.), von Dr. Ines Konzcak-Nagel zu den Kopien der Wandmalereien von Kizil des Künstlers Han Rakyeon mit Begeisterung aufgenommen. Die Recherchen von Dr. Corinna Wessels-Mevissen zur Biographie und zur kunsthistorischen Einordnung eines „abwesenden" Sammlungsobjekts – Der gandharische „Pensive Bodhisattva", angekauft 1910, und die neuesten Forschungsergebnisse von Dr. Gudrun Melzer zur Kulturgeschichte aus Gandhara anhand von Manuskriptfunden lösten ebenfalls angeregte Diskussionen aus.

Ähnlich intensiv war der Austausch mit der wissenschaftlichen Community bei den von der Dunhuang Foundation und der University of Cambridge (Prof. Imre Galambos) angebotenen virtuellen Lectures zur Seidenstraße, zu denen die GIAK-Mitglieder freundlicherweise eingeladen wurden. Abgerundet wurde dieses thematisch weitgefächerte Programm durch Kuratorenführungen im Humboldt Forum von Dr. Lilla Russel-Smith und Martina Stoye. Nach Lockerung der Coronamaßnahmen fand die im Mai 2022 von Dr. Caren Dreyer organisierte Exkursion nach Leipzig mit Besuch des Grassi Museums besonders großen Anklang und auch die GIAK-Mitgliederversammlung konnte wieder analog stattfinden. Beides erfreute sich reger Teilnahme ebenso wie der im Vortragsraum des Asiatischen Museums gehaltene Vortrag von Dr. Michael Henss „Rituale und Ritual Objekte im tibetischen Buddhismus". Im Anschluss daran wurde im lauschigen Ambiente der Luise die Sommerpause eingeläutet, besonders ausgelassen und voller Erwartung auf die anstehende Eröffnung des Ostflügels des Humboldt Forums.

Für das Museum gingen auch nach der Eröffnung im Herbst 2021 umfangreiche Umzugsmaßnahmen weiter. Zwei weitere große Ausstellungssäle wurden für die Eröffnung der Ostspange im Herbst 2022 eingerichtet. Im Kubusraum Süd wurde die Einrichtung der Himalaya-Galerie abgeschlossen und letzte Halterungen und Texte eingebracht. Im unteren Teil dieser Studiensammlung ist die Höhle der ringtragenden Tauben, die von Holger Manzke restauratorisch bearbeitet wurde, zu sehen. Die hohen Wände des Ausstellungsraumes zieren die beeindruckenden Wandmalereien aus Zentralasien (**Abb. 1**). Sie bekamen letzte Retuschen durch die freiberuflichen Restauratoren der Fa. Lenzner & Gramann. Andere Malereien, die durch die Restauratorenteams Katrin König, Marie Fortmann, Daniela Arnold und Kathrin Manzke-Leubner restauriert wurden, trafen im Frühjahr 2022 als letzte Glanzstücke im Humboldt Forum ein. Die zweite noch fertigzustellende Ausstellungsfläche war die Galerie für Südostasien, die geprägt ist durch die Installation der Abgüsse der Flachreliefs aus Angkor Wat. Zahlreiche Bronzen und Skulpturen aus Thailand (**Abb. 2**), Kambodscha und Myanmar, die im Vorjahr in Dahlem sorgsam verpackt wurden, erhielten nun ihren Platz in den Vitrinen im Humboldt Forum.

Der Dauerbetrieb des Museums für Asiatische Kunst im Humboldt Forum lief mit einigen Nachbesserungen an der Haustechnik und den umfänglichen Arbeitsprozessen an. Die Werkstätten der Restauratoren waren intensiv ausgelastet. Parallel dazu galt es, in Dahlem noch große Konvolute der Sammlungen an chinesischer und japanischer Malerei, Keramik und Lackkunst zu verpacken, die ebenso wie die indische Miniaturmalerei im Humboldt Forum als Studiensammlung in den Depoträumen verwahrt werden. Ein Umzug von nochmal mehreren tausend Kunstwerken, der neben dem bereits laufenden Ausstellungsbetrieb umgesetzt wurde. Für die Mitarbeiter, die nun zwischen zwei Standorten pendelten, eine logistische und zeitliche Herausforderung. Hinzu kam besonders für die Sammlungs-

Abb. 1 Einrichtung des Kubus Süd mit Wandmalereien der nördlichen Seidenstraße © Staatliche Museen zu Berlin, Museum für Asiatische Kunst / Uta Schröder

verwaltung die digitale Verstandortung von insgesamt ca. 10.000 Sammlungsobjekten.

In Dahlem war mit den stattfindenden Kunsttransporten und Verpackungskampagnen weiterhin viel Bewegung. Hinzu kam der nun langsam wieder sich normalisierende Leihverkehr. Ab Oktober zeigt das Lindenmuseum in Stuttgart einige Leihgaben aus der Sammlung südindischer Kunst in der Sonderausstellung „Von Liebe und Krieg“ (siehe Anzeige).

Zum Stichwort Erwerbungen schätzt sich das Museum glücklich über ein Konvolut an historischen Fotografien aus Indien aus dem 19. Jh. Außerdem hat das Haus ein besonders beeindruckendes Schränkchen aus der Moghulzeit als Dauerleihgabe erhalten.

Ein interessantes Projekt soll noch genannt werden, das sich der Erforschung der thailändischen Handschriften in unserer Sammlung widmet. In gemeinsamer Kooperation konnte das Museum unter der Projektleitung von Martina Stoye, Kuratorin für Süd- und Südostasiatische Kunst und dem Asien-Afrika Institut der Universität Hamburg, hier Dr. Peera Panarut, Professor Dr. Volker Grabowsky und Sutheera Satayaphan, 70 Handschriften erforschen und digitalisieren (**Abb. 3**).[1]

Auch die Digitalisierung der historischen Erwerbungsbücher des Hauses sowie der gesamten Staatlichen Museen zu Berlin sind eine Errungenschaft, die weitere Forschungen nun auch online ermöglichen.[2] Des Weiteren ist eine größere Maßnahme zur Digitalisierung und Visualisierung objektbezogener Daten (MDVOS) ange-

1 https://www.smb.museum/museen-einrichtungen/museum-fuer-asiatische-kunst/sammeln-forschen/forschung.

2 https://www.smb.museum/nachrichten/detail/online-publikation-staatliche-museen-zu-berlin-veroeffentlichen-historische-erwerbungsbuecher.

Abb. 2 Einrichtung der Inszenierung thailändischer Bronzen in der Galerie für Südostasitische Kunst © Staatliche Museen zu Berlin, Museum für Asiatische Kunst / Uta Schröder

laufen, die zukünftig auch den Onlinekatalog der asiatischen Sammlungen erweitern wird.[3]

Bereits im letzten Jahr hat Frau Kerstin Pinther als Kuratorin für zeitgenössische Kunst ihre Tätigkeit im Museum aufgenommen. Zudem bereichern als feste Restauratoren Ulrike Stelzer und Sebastian Kolberg das Museum. Friederike Weis führt das Projekt zu Indischen Alben der zweiten Hälfte des achtzehnten Jahrhunderts am Museum fort[4] und schließlich forscht Frau Birgit Schmidt im Rahmen ihrer Dissertation zu den Lehmskulpturen aus Zentralasien.

Dörte Eriskat & Uta Schröder

Abb. 3 Projektteilnehmer (v.l.n.r.) Dr. Peera Panarut, Sutheera Satayaphan (Universität Hamburg) und Martina Stoye, Patrik Held (Museum für Asiatische Kunst) bei der Sichtung eines thailändischen Manuskriptes. © Staatliche Museen zu Berlin, Museum für Asiatische Kunst / Uta Schröder

3 https://www.smb.museum/museen-einrichtungen/ethnologisches-museum/sammeln-forschen/forschung/massnahme-zur-digitalisierung-und-visualisierung-objektbezogener-daten-mdvos/.

4 https://www.smb.museum/museen-einrichtungen/museum-fuer-asiatische-kunst/sammeln-forschen/forschung/indische-alben-der-zweiten-haelfte-des-18-jahrhunderts/.

Autoren / Contributors

Thomas Arens (Dipl. Rest. FH-Köln), ist seit 2015 im Museum für Asiatische Kunst als Textilrestaurator tätig.
<t.arens@smb.spk-berlin.de>

Dr. Dörte Eriskat, Historikerin, Studium der Geschichts-, Politik- und Rechtswissenschaften in Zürich, Edinburgh und Trier, Promotion in den Fächern Geschichte u. Politikwissenschaft an der Universität Trier. Derzeit Forschungen zur mittelalterlichen textilen Kultur der Stadt Luxemburg und zur Wirtschafts- und Textilgeschichte: Europe through Textiles: Network for an integrated and interdisciplinary Humanities (EuroWeb). Schatzmeisterin der GIAK.
<deriskat@aol.de>

Dipl. Rest. Marie Fortmann, 2004–2005 Restaurierungsvorpraktikum in Berlin; 2005–2011 Studium der Kunsttechnologie, Konservierung und Restaurierung von Wandmalerei und Architekturfarbigkeit an der Hochschule für Bildende Künste Dresden; seit 2011 freiberufliche Diplomrestauratorin für Wandmalerei und Architekturfarbigkeit; Konservierungen und Restaurierungen u.a. in Kirchen, Schlössern und verschiedenen UNESCO-Weltkulturerbestätten in Deutschland, 2017–2022 Konservierungen und Restaurierungen asiatischer und islamischer Wandmalereien des Museums für Asiatische Kunst, Berlin, und des Museums für Islamische Kunst, Berlin.
<post@mf-restaurierung.de>

Raffael Dedo Gadebusch ist wissenschaftlicher Koordinator der Asiatischen Kunstsammlungen im Humboldt Forum und seit 1.10. 2018 Leiter des Museums für Asiatische Kunst, Berlin. Als Stellvertretender Direktor und Kurator des Museums für Indische Kunst und (seit 2006) des Museums für Asiatische Kunst hat er eine Vielzahl von Ausstellungen zur Kunst Südasiens im In- und Ausland kuratiert. Schwerpunkte seiner kuratorischen Arbeit und seiner breit gefächerten Publikationstätigkeit sind neben der indo-islamischen Kunst die moderne und zeitgenössische Kunst sowie die Fotografie des 19. und 20. Jahrhunderts in Südasien.
<r.gadebusch@smb.spk-berlin.de>

Univ.-Prof. i.R. Dr. Adalbert J. Gail, geboren 1941; 1968 Promotion an der Ludwig-Maximilians-Universität, München; 1972–1973 Wissenschaftlicher Mitarbeiter am Museum für Indische Kunst Berlin; 1978 Habilitation für Indische Philologie und Indische Kunstgeschichte an der Freien Universität Berlin; 1974–2006 Professor für Indische Kunstgeschichte an der FU Berlin; Dekan am Fachbereich Altertumswissenschaften der FU von 1989 bis 1991; seit 1995 Gastprofessor an der Philosophischen Fakultät der Karls-Universität Prag; 2006–2014 Lehraufträge an der FU Berlin; seit 2015 Angkor-Forschung: „Hinduismus – Pantheon und Ikonographie".
<adalbert.gail@fu-berlin.de>

Dr. Gerald Kozicz, geboren 1966 in Graz; beschäftigt sich seit mehr als zwanzig Jahren mit Themen der Architektur und Kulturgeschichte des westlichen Himalayas; derzeit Projektleiter eines vom österreichischen Fonds zur Förderung der wissenschaftlichen Forschung (FWF) geförderten Projekts zur Dokumentation des kulturellen Erbes von Chamba (Himachal Pradesh) am Institut für Architektur und Medien der Technischen Universität Graz.
<gerald.kozicz@gmx.at>

Dorina Michaelis M.A. studied South Asian Art History, East Asian Art History and Archaeology of the ancient Near East at the Freie Universität Berlin. Until 2019 she was a Curatorial Assistant at the Museum für Islamische Kunst, curating the exhibition "The Colours of Sindh". She currently works as a freelance art historian with an emphasis on exhibitions and digitization of museum collection. Her research focusses on glazed ceramics and crafts from South Asia, particularly from the 18th to early 20th century.
<dorinamichaelis@gmx.de>

Dipl. Rest. Angela Mitschke, 2008–2014 Studium der Kunsttechnologie, Konservierung und Restaurierung von Wandmalerei und Architekturfarbigkeit an der Hochschule für Bildende Künste Dresden; Diplomarbeit über ein Wandmalereiobjekt am Museum für Asiatische Kunst, Berlin; zwischen 2010 und 2017 mehrere Aufenthalte in Ladakh

(Indien) für projektbezogene Arbeit an Wandmalereien in buddhistischen Tempeln; von 2015 bis 2021 freiberufliche Restauratorin; seit 2021 Vorstandsmitglied der Achi Association Schweiz und wissenschaftliches Volontariat am Landesdenkmalamt Berlin.

<a.mitschke@mailbox.org>

Prof. Dr. Alexis von Poser ist stellvertretender Direktor des Ethnologischen Museums und des Museums für Asiatische Kunst der Staatlichen Museen zu Berlin, Honorarprofessor für Im/materielle Kulturen an der Freien Universität Berlin und aktuell einer der beiden Sprecher*innen des Forschungscampus Dahlem. Er hat umfassende Forschungserfahrung in Papua-Neuguinea und Lehrerfahrungen an Universitäten in Berlin (FU), Göttingen, Hannover, Heidelberg und Madang (Papua-Neuguinea). Seine Tätigkeiten an Museen in Berlin, Hannover und Lübeck waren und sind verbunden mit reicher Forschungs-, Ausstellungs- und Publikationstätigkeit. Er ist Mitherausgeber der Zeitschrift für Ethnologie – Journal of Social and Cultural Anthropology, sowie des Baessler-Archivs.

<A.vonPoser@smb.spk-berlin.de>

Prof. Dr. Patricia Rahemipour ist Direktorin des Instituts für Museumsforschung der Staatlichen Museen zu Berlin und aktuell eine der beiden Sprecher*innen des Forschungscampus Dahlem. Besonderer Schwerpunkt und reichlich Erfahrung liegen im kuratorischen Bereich. Intensive Forschungstätigkeiten im Bereich der Museums Studies. Nach ihrer Tätigkeit als Leiterin der Lehrsammlung am Lehrstuhl für Ur- und Frühgeschichte an der Universität Leipzig, arbeitete sie u.a. als Projektleiterin und leitende Kuratorin für das Deutsche Archäologische Institut und das Exzellenzcluster Topoi, an der Römisch-Germanischen Kommission, am Jüdischen Museum Frankfurt, sowie am Botanischen Garten Berlin, wo sie die Leitung des Botanischen Museums und der Abteilung Wissenskommunikation übernahm.

<P.Rahemipour@smb.spk-berlin.de>

Dipl. Rest. Joana Schaer, 1997–2000 Restaurierungsvorpraktikum u.a. am Landesdenkmalamt Berlin, dreimonatiger Italienaufenthalt in Padova (Leonardo da Vinci-Programm Bereich Restaurierung); 2000–2003 Studium Lehramt Gymnasium Kunst/Italienisch an der Hochschule für Kunst und Design Burg Giebichenstein und an der Martin-Luther-Universität in Halle/Saale; 2003 Studium der Kunsttechnologie, Konservierung und Restaurierung von Wandmalerei und Architekturfarbigkeit an der Hochschule für Bildende Künste in Dresden, Diplom 2010; seitdem als freiberufliche Restauratorin tätig; Ende 2017 – Februar 2022 freie Mitarbeit an verschiedenen Restaurierungsprojekten am Museum für Asiatische Kunst, Berlin.

<joana.schaer@posteo.de>

Dr. Uta Schröder, Kunsthistorikerin für Südasien, Studium der Indischen Kunstgeschichte, Indischen Philologie und Ethnologie an der Freien Universität Berlin, Promotion 2016; 2016–2017 wissenschaftliche Museumsassistentin i.F. am Museum für Asiatische Kunst Berlin; seit 2018 Sammlungsverwalterin für den Umzug in das Humboldt Forum. Redaktion und Lektorat der Indo-Asiatischen Zeitschrift seit 2018.

<uta_schroeder@yahoo.de>

Mercedes Tortorici studied art history and art management at the Universidad del Salvador in Buenos Aires, Argentina, where she also worked as an assistant teacher for five years. In Germany she completed the master *Religion und Philosophie in Asien* at the Ludwig-Maximilian Universität in Munich. She wrote her master thesis on the visual language of the Ajanta wall paintings. She is currently a PhD student at the Universität Leipzig under the supervision of Prof. Monika Zin, researching on the depiction of women on the Ajanta wall paintings.

<mtortorici@gmail.com>

Dr. Corinna Wessels-Mevissen is a specialist in South Asian art and archaeology based in Berlin. She has worked as a curator, taught several university courses, and she has one monograph, some edited volumes and a number of research articles to her credit.

<corinnawessels@yahoo.de>

Ji Ho Yi, born in 1984 in Seoul, Republic of Korea; studied Economics and Art History at Seoul National University, South Korea, from 2003 to 2008; and completed her M.A. in Art History at Seoul National University from 2008 to 2012. She worked between 2012 and 2013 at the Kyujanggak Institute of Korean Studies as a manager of the exhibition space. Moving to Germany in 2014, Ji Ho Yi attended courses at the Institut für Indologie und Tibetologie at Ludwig-Maximilians-Universität in Munich as a guest student for a few years until she moved to Leipzig in 2018. Since November 2018, Ji Ho Yi is studying under the supervision of Prof. Dr. Monika Zin at the Universität Leipzig. She works as a PhD student in the project group "Buddhist Murals of Kucha on the Northern Silk Road" at the Sächsische Akademie der Wissenschaften zu Leipzig since March 2019.

<joie1110@gmail.com>

Gesellschaft für indo-asiatische Kunst, Berlin e.V.

Vorstand / Board

Erster Vorsitzender: Prof. Dr. Felix Gross
Zweite Vorsitzende: Dr. Caren Dreyer
Dr. Ines Konczak-Nagel
Schatzmeisterin: Dr. Dörte Eriskat
Schriftführerin: Elisabeth Ruhe

Ehrenmitglieder / Honorary Members

Dr. Dietrich Mahlo, Berlin
Prof. Dr. Christian Schwarz-Schilling, Bundesminister a.D., Büdingen
Dipl.-Ing. Gerd J.R. Mevissen, Berlin
Elke Jacob, Berlin

Mitglieder / Members 2022

(Gesamtzahl: **150**; Fördermitglieder in Fettdruck)

Achinger, Ernst Rudolf, Berlin
Ande, Dipl.-Ing. Diethard, Bangkok, Thailand
Arlt, Robert, Berlin
Augustin, Dr. Bernd, Hamburg
Bär, Elisabeth, Berlin
Berenburg-Dorow, Dr. Dagmar, Berlin
Berg, Jessica, Berlin
Bhattacharjee, Edda, Frankfurt/Main
Bhattacharya-Haesner, Dr. Chhaya, Berlin
Bickelmann, Eckehard, Heidelberg
Biermann, Dr. h.c. Hans, Berlin
Biermann, Simon, Berlin
Blumenstock, Dr. Erich, Frankfurt/Main
Böhm, Christine, Berlin
Bossecker, Michael, Potsdam
Brandhoff, Eckart, München
Broeskamp, Bernadette, Berlin
Brühl, Hasso, Berlin
Brunner-Mattenberger, Elsa, Zürich, Schweiz
Bülow, Gabriele von, Berlin
Buschmann, Ines, Berlin
Camargo, Sofia, Berlin
Debes, Helga, Berlin
Deuchert, Dr. Norbert A., Heidelberg
Dorow, Dr. Rainer, Berlin
Dreyer, Dr. Caren, Berlin
Ehrhard, Prof. Dr. Franz-Karl, Heidelberg
Eichner, Ingrid, Berlin
Eriskat, Dr. Dörte, Berlin
Feiler, Dr. Leander A., Riemerling
Feistel, Dr. Hartmut-Ortwin, Berlin
Felten, Dr. Wolfgang, München

Fußmann, Prof. Klaus, Berlin

Gadebusch, Raffael Dedo, Berlin

Gail, Prof. Dr. Adalbert J., Berlin

Ganguli, Dr. Indranil, Berlin

Garland, Prof. Dr. Marc, USA

Gerfelmeyer, Dr. Gerhard, Bremerhaven

Gilge, Christina, Berlin (Kassenprüferin)

Glanz-Baumann, Barbara, Berlin

Götz, Alexander, Vietnam

Gross, Prof. Dr. Felix, Berlin

Habighorst, Prof. Dr. med. Ludwig, Koblenz

Hadjinicolaou, Yannis, Berlin

Hansen, Günter, Berlin

Hardt, Peter, Radevormwald

Hartmann, Dr. Oliver, Berlin

Hatzl, Michael, München

Hegewald, Prof. Dr. Julia A.B., Bonn

Helbig (ehem. Heinrich), Julia, Beelitz

Henkel, Dr. Robert, Overijse, Belgien

Henrici, Dr. Hans, Köln

Henss, Dr. Michael, Zürich, Schweiz

Hoesch, Dr. Henning, Düren-Hoven

Hohn, Dr. Kai-Torsten, Straelen

Jacob, Bernd-Peter, Berlin

Jacob, Elke, Berlin (Kassenprüferin)

Jäschke, Susanne, Bramsche

Jagiella, Olivia, Berlin

Kaht, Dr. Hilmar, Berlin

Kaht, Hsiao-li, Berlin

Kapp, Miriam, Berlin

Karino, Dr. Satomi (Hiyama), Tokyo, Japan

Kelterborn, Angela, Berlin

Klaeden, Eckhart von, MdB, Hildesheim

Klohe, Hans-Werner, Berlin

Köllner, Helmut, München

Koelnsperger, Ernst W., München

Konczak-Nagel, Dr. Ines, Berlin

Kozicz, Dr. Gerald, Graz, Österreich

Krieger, Karl, Makati City, Philippinen

Krüger, Dr. Patrick F., Bochum

Kuhl, Rainer, Berlin

Kuhn, Ruth, Berlin

Leisen, Prof. Dr. Hans, Köln

Lindner, Dr. Andreas, München

Lobo, Dr. Wibke, Berlin

Luczanits, Prof. Dr. Christian, London, UK

Mahlo, Dr. Dietrich, Berlin

Mahlo, Sophie, Berlin

Maier, Hermann, Rosenheim

Majewski, Kai-Michael, Berlin

Mangold, Rani, Berlin

Melzer, Dr. Gudrun, München

Mevissen, Dipl.-Ing. Gerd J.R., Berlin

Michaelis, Dorina, Berlin

Müller, Dr. Wolfram H., Berlin

Myint, Dr. med. Tin Than, Enfield, UK

Nahrwold, Lena, Berlin

Neumann, Reinhard, Berlin

Otteni, Willi J., Hamburg

Ottleben, Dr. Holger, Berlin

Paulmann, Hanna, Darmstadt

Poncar, Prof. Dr. Jaroslav, Köln

Port, Thomas, Berlin

Reichart, Prof. Dr. Peter A., Berlin

Reichelt, Hans-Jürgen, Balge †

Reichstein, Reinhard, Borgsdorf

Robbins, Dr. Kenneth X., Potomac, USA

Rößler, Peter, München

Ruhe, Elisabeth, Wustermark

Ruitenbeek, Prof. Dr. Klaas, Berlin

Russell-Smith, Dr. Lilla, Berlin

Sander, Dr. Lore, Berlin

Schenz, Frank, Luxemburg

Schmidt, Birgit Angelika, Berlin

Schröder-Göcke, Sylvia, Hamburg

Schröder, Dr. Uta, Brandenburg

Schwarz-Schilling, Prof. Dr. Christian, Bundesminister a.D., Büdingen

Schwarz-Schilling, Marie-Luise, Büdingen

Segond, Karim, Berlin

Seiffert, Albert, Nürnberg

Seitz, Dr. Konrad, Botschafter a.D., Wachtberg-Pech

Sengebusch, Bodo, Berlin

Souchon, Jacqueline, Berlin

Souchon, Prof. Dr. med. Rainer, Berlin

Speidel, Markus, Prof. em., Brimersdorf, Schweiz

Spuhler, Dr. Friedrich, Potsdam-Babelsberg

Stosch, Michael, Eisenach

Sun-Torsten, Jennifer, Berlin

ten Feld, Hans, Berlin

Thiele, Prof. Dr. Peter, Berlin

Thinius, Carola, Berlin

Thinius, Rolf, Berlin

Torsten, PD Dr. Uwe, Berlin

Uken, Sybille, Berlin

Venzke, Günter, Berlin

Von der Lahr, Evelyne, Villeneuve, Schweiz

Von der Lahr, Joachim, Villeneuve, Schweiz

Waldschmidt, Dr. Rainer, Wetzlar

Wang, Junwen, Schanghai, China

Wang, Dr. Ching-Ling, Amsterdam, Niederlande

Weinmann, Dr. Gisela, Berlin

Weis, Dr. Friederike, Berlin

Weise, Kati, Berlin

Welge, Pieter K.G., Wolfenbüttel

Whitfield, Dr. Mirko, Tübingen-Pfrondorf

Win Maung (Thampawady), Mandalay, Myanmar

Winter, Anja, Berlin

Woeste, Dr. Cordula, Berlin

Wörner, Michael, Bangkok, Thailand

Wolf, Efram Jasper, Berlin

Yi, Ji Ho, Leipzig

Zin, Prof. Dr. Monika, München

Zwiener, Thorsten, Essen

Zylka, Dr. rer.nat. Renate, Berlin

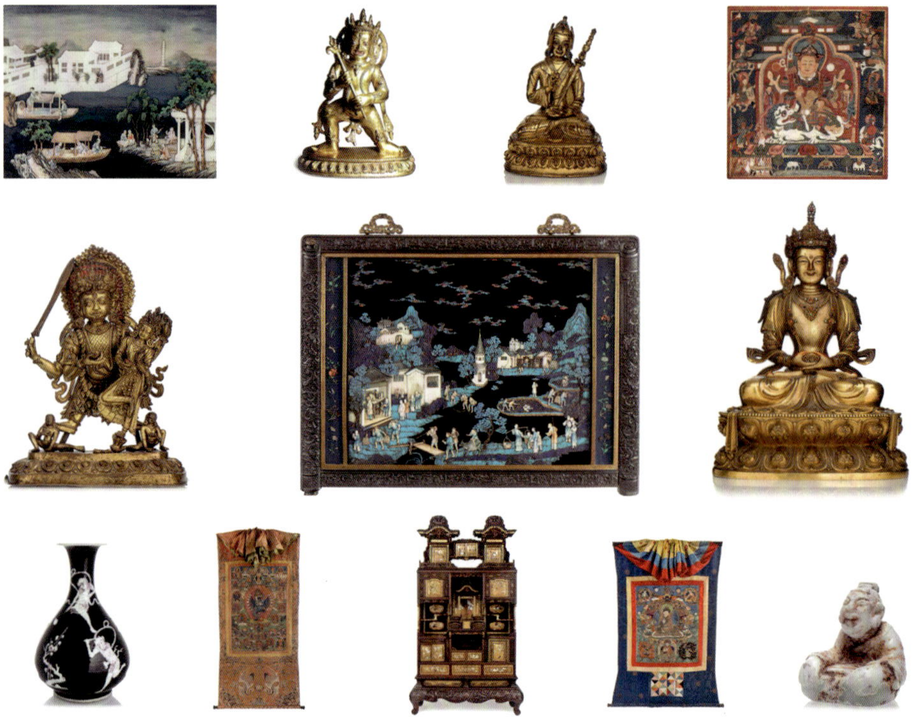

Tamilische Geschichte(n) aus Indien und der Welt
LINDEN-MUSEUM STUTTGART
Staatliches Museum für Völkerkunde
Von Liebe und Krieg
Gefördert von:
Baden-Württemberg
MINISTERIUM FÜR WISSENSCHAFT, FORSCHUNG UND KUNST
8.10.2022 – 7.5.2023
Linden-Museum Stuttgart

Sind Sie schon Mitglied der Gesellschaft für indo-asiatische Kunst?
Informieren Sie sich auf unserer Webseite über unseren aktiven Freundeskreis und geniessen die Vorteile einer Mitgliedschaft.
GIAK.ORG
GESELLSCHAFT FÜR INDO-ASIATISCHE KUNST BERLIN E.V
c/o Museum für Asiatische Kunst | E-Mail: info@giak.org

Indo-Asiatische Zeitschrift

Mitteilungen der Gesellschaft für indo-asiatische Kunst

26 · 2022

IMPRESSUM / IMPRINT	*Indo-Asiatische Zeitschrift. Mitteilungen der Gesellschaft für indo-asiatische Kunst.* ISSN 1434-8829. © 2022 Gesellschaft für indo-asiatische Kunst Berlin e.V. (Herausgeber). Website: http://www.giak.org Die *Indo-Asiatische Zeitschrift* erscheint jährlich. Mitglieder erhalten die Publikation kostenlos, für Nichtmitglieder beträgt der Preis EUR 19,80. Ältere Ausgaben sind über die unten genannte Bezugsadresse erhältlich.
Redaktion / Editing	Dr. Uta Schröder, Dr. Ines Konczak-Nagel, Gerd J.R. Mevissen, Raffael Dedo Gadebusch
Wissenschaftliche Berater	Dr. Caren Dreyer
Lektorat / Editing	Dr. Uta Schröder, Dr. Ines Konczak-Nagel
Satz / Layout	Rainer Kuhl, EB-Verlag Dr. Brandt
ISBN	978-3-86893-427-4
Herstellung und Druck / Manufacturing & print	Druckhaus Sportflieger, Berlin
Bezugsadresse/ Copies available from	EB-Verlag Dr. Brandt, Jägerstraße 47, 13595 Berlin Tel. (030) 68977233, Fax (030) 91607774 post@ebverlag.de | www.ebverlag.de Museum für Asiatische Kunst, Kunstsammlung Süd-, Südost- und Zentralasien, Takustraße 40, D-14195 Berlin, Tel. (030) 8301-361, Fax (030) 8301-502, E-mail: info@giak.org
Umschlagabbildung / Front Cover Image	Kopf einer Devata, Lehmskulptur, 32 x 20 x 15 cm, Statuenhöhle, Kizil, Xinjiang (Autonomes Gebiet), China; Museum für Asiatische Kunst Inv.-Nr. III 7881. (c) Staatliche Museen zu Berlin, Museum für Asiatische Kunst